"Land's hushed, agonized prose propels this story relentlessly . . . through the blasted landscape of the cult of American masculinity. . . . The tale throws sparks of delicious dissonance, hums with righteous *frisson*."   —*The San Diego Union-Tribune*

"Superb . . . From now on the definition [of *hazing*] should simply read: see Brad Land's memoir, *Goat*."   —*Newsweek*

"Spare and brutal . . . a startling picture of accepted cruelty and a haunting look inside the mind of a victim."
                    —*The Plain Dealer* (Cleveland)

"This dark, brutal story is told so plainly and vividly—with the literary equivalent of breathlessness—that it gathers momentum until the very end, when it finally leaves you feeling as though a tornado had just passed by. . . . [It's] one whirlwind of a book."
                    —*Fort Worth Star-Telegram*

"Land touches the raw bone of some hard truths. . . . The subterranean connections glimpsed in Land's experience emerge with agonizing honesty."   —*The Onion*

"*Goat* should be required reading for every scared, isolated, naïve teenage boy who thinks that joining a fraternity might solve his problems. And required reading for anyone who's ever loved someone they didn't understand."
                    —THISBE NISSEN, author of *The Good People of New York*

"Intense, well-measured prose . . . unconventional . . . This book is potent."   —*Tulsa World*

"Land's debut is probably this spring's memoir with the strongest buzz, one that blazes a searing trail in what seems a new memoir subject area—violence among men against men."
                    —*Seattle Post-Intelligencer*

"A starkly written, haunting account of coming-of-age rituals for young men among the South's middle class . . . *Goat* is a story of hope and courage."   —*The Charlotte Observer*

"For those victims unwittingly denied a voice, the memoir becomes a necessary means of reclaiming it. . . . Land does a wonderful job of exposing the hyper-masculine, booze-soaked world of the fraternity, one in which any emotions besides anger and lust are derided."
                                  —*News & Record* (Greensboro, North Carolina)

"A cross between *Animal House* and *Deliverance,* Brad Land's memoir is a brass-knuckled rebuke of the fraternity system and its sado-masochistic rites of passage. . . . But *Goat* is more than a revenge piece. In disquieting detail and mercilessly spare language, it traces the degenerative effect of violence on a youthful sensibility."
                                  —*The Miami Herald*

"*Goat* is a heartfelt look at how violence can poison young men's lives."   —*People*

"Raw . . . beguiling and beautiful . . . raw-boned but controlled . . . [*Goat*] examines not only the wellsprings of violence, but its reservoirs. . . . Land's language is clipped and spare, yet potent."
                                  —*The Post and Courier* (Charleston, South Carolina)

"Boys will be boys, and sometimes that's a dangerous thing to be. That's one of the lessons of Brad Land's unsettling memoir. . . . Written with a novelist's finesse."   —*San Jose Mercury News*

"Land probes the underbelly of fraternity life . . . , and it's about time: This whole brotherhood business is ripe, fascinating material. . . . *Goat* casts an eerie spell."   —*Newsday*

"In a voice that's bare-to-the-bone vulnerable, Land glues you to each wince-inducing page."   —*New York Post*

"Land's recounting of the actual traumatic events, written in clipped, matter-of-fact prose, is well wrought and affecting."
                                  —*San Francisco Chronicle*

"There have been a few great memoirs in the throng that have been published since creative nonfiction became a hot genre. Mary Karr's *The Liar's Club* is one. Land's *Goat* stands ready to take its place next to that harrowing tale. It is notable for Land's impeccable prose, for his verbal and emotional integrity, and for speaking to a rare subject—the hearts and minds of tough young guys—rough on the outside but tender at the core."   —*Colorado Springs Independent*

"Powerful . . . The best survivor memoirs offer a scrupulously honest rendering of both the writer's powerful feelings and the disquieting events that led to them. . . . [Land's] fierce prose . . . acts as the ideal counterweight to his own vulnerability. The tension between Land's tough style and his fragile state of mind has produced an emotionally charged work."   —*Nashville Scene*

"This is the most astonishing debut I've ever read. *Goat* is beguiling, brutal, and tender at once. By giving us an honest portrait of the love between brothers, Brad Land holds up a mirror to the lie of false fraternity."   —HAVEN KIMMEL, author of *A Girl Named Zippy*

"[*Goat*] is so self-assured, you won't be able to stop reading."
     —*Esquire*

"The enigmatic long-term responses to systematic acts of brutality propel Brad Land's *Goat*. . . . [Land's sentences] have the rhythm of panicked breathing. . . . Visceral . . . potent."   —*The Village Voice*

"Brutal . . . Land's literary voice is stark and distant."
     —*New York* magazine

"Written with a heart seared with pain and a pen filled with passion, Brad Land's tale is street-fight brutal and gut-wrench tragic. It is a book that every teenager should read and every parent must read, especially those of us with sons. *Goat* never lets go. It rips and shreds us with blade-sharp dialogue and a relentless pace, all the while exposing the bravest of souls and the most gentle of hearts."
     —LORENZO CARCATERRA, author of *Gangster* and *Street Boys*

"Harrowing . . . the spring's most promising memoir."

—*Entertainment Weekly*

"Land's clipped prose lends this memoir a feeling of immediacy, and he adds novelistic weight to simple, almost primitive dialogue."

—*Booklist*

"Taut . . . vicious."

—*Elle*

"Land . . . writes with artistry and gives meaning to the violence, in turn speaking to the darkest side of American life. . . . This is one of those impossible-to-put-down books. . . . This will be widely read as one of the first books about assaults on men."

—*Library Journal* (starred review)

"Jarring . . . furiously told . . . Land's punches hit home: Every man, in some capacity, has been there."

—*Men's Journal*

"With a uniquely hip narrative style, gritty with plenty of heart . . . [*Goat* is] immensely readable. . . . Land's tough yet tender book speaks to the fears and isolation of young alienated adults with compelling power, candor and compassion."

—*Publishers Weekly* (starred review)

"How Land can stand to revisit these miseries with such delirious pungency would be a wonder, except that his sense of relief at having survived them is palpable. Fine, grim work." —*Kirkus Reviews*

G O A T

Random House Trade Paperbacks New York

G O A T

A Memoir

B r a d   L a n d

2005 Random House Trade Paperback Edition
Copyright © 2004 by Brad Land
Reading group guide copyright © 2005 by Random House, Inc.

Published in the United States by Random House Trade Paperbacks, an imprint of The Random House Publishing Group, a division of Random House, Inc., New York.

RANDOM HOUSE TRADE PAPERBACKS and colophon are registered trademarks of Random House, Inc.

Originally published in hardcover in the United States by Random House, an imprint of The Random House Publishing Group, a division of Random House, Inc., in 2004.

Grateful acknowledgment is made to BOA Editions, Ltd., c/o The Permissions Company for permission to reprint an excerpt from "Song" from *Song* by Brigit Pegeen Kelly, copyright © 1995 by Brigit Pegeen Kelly. Reprinted with the permission of BOA Editions, Ltd.

Library of Congress Cataloging-in-Publication Data
Land, Brad.
Goat : a memoir / Brad Land.
p.   cm.
ISBN 0-8129-6968-5
1. Land, Brad. 2. Youth—South Carolina—Biography. 3. South Carolina—Social life and customs. 4. Violence—South Carolina. I. Title.
HQ799.2.V56L36 2004
305.235'092—dc21
[B]
2003047067

Printed in the United States of America
Random House website address: www.atrandom.com
2 4 6 8 9 7 5 3 1
Book design by JoAnne Metsch

For Brett

Part One

Yes lady, that is what I said. Goat.

CORMAC MCCARTHY, *Blood Meridian*

But listen: here is the point. The boys thought to have
Their fun and be done with it. It was harder work than they
Had imagined, this silly sacrifice, but they finished the job,
Whistling as they washed their large hands in the dark.
What they didn't know was that the goat's head was already
Singing behind them in the tree. What they didn't know
Was that the goat's head would go on singing, just for them,
Long after the ropes were down, and that they would learn to listen,
Pail after pail, stroke after patient stroke. They would
Wake in the night thinking they heard the wind in the trees
Or a night bird, but their hearts beating harder. There
Would be a whistle, a hum, a high murmur, and, at last, a song,
The low song a lost boy sings remembering his mother's call.
Not a cruel song, no no, not cruel at all. This song
Is sweet. It is sweet. The heart dies of this sweetness.

BRIGIT PEGEEN KELLY, "Song"

THIS IS HOW IT GOES:

We're getting floored at a beginning-of-the-semester party. Me, my younger brother Brett, these three people we came with. At this old fraternity house. Two stories with a big front porch and a backyard with a chain-link fence.

Brett's on the porch standing next to me. People moving all over the place. Like cells. Everything pulsing. All sweat and smoke. The house is breathing.

These two girls come up. Just stand there looking us over. One of the girls looks at Brett like she loves him already. She's short and has long hair pulled into a ponytail. Legs all muscled like a soccer player's. She's wearing a Zeppelin T-shirt with a hole beneath the neck cuff. The other girl's standing beside her all bucktoothed and shaky. Got a tattoo on her left shoulder blade. Something swirled and tribal. Her arms crossed. I give her a smoke and she nods, cups one hand around the lighter I hold out and I can tell she's drunk by the way her eyes wobble,

the way she squints them against the porch lights. The other
girl rubs the shaky one's back, runs her hand down and pauses
in the bare patch of skin between her jeans and top. The shaky
girl looks her over and smiles. Brett tells them to kiss. They
look at each other and laugh and then the shaky girl moves
toward the other one, puts a hand around her waist and holds
the cigarette out to the side. Her tongue's out and inside the
other's mouth and they lock together, wet cheeks pulsing with
the overhead light. The shaky one steps back and pulls on the
smoke, exhales and looks at Brett. I'm staring at the two girls
and the shaky girl asks if that was okay, and Brett says yeah
that was cool, and I nod, say yeah good, and then Brett says do
it again and they just laugh. The short girl says you don't even
know us and Brett says so and cocks back his beer. When he
brings it down, she takes the beer from Brett and drinks. Hands
it back. And now the shaky girl looks at me like she knows
something about me with my skinny arms and black hair all
matted from the hot air outside. Brett's talking to the short girl
and I don't know what to say with this shaky one staring at me.
The short one leans, whispers in her friend's ear. They turn and
walk away.

Brett tells me they want us to come over later.

I nod like it's standard.

SCHOOL'S TWO DAYS away, and for both Brett and me, it's
the whole college-in-the-same-town-you-went-to-high-school-
in thing. It'll be my second year, Brett's first, and right now I'm
not too happy with this small liberal arts school because it's

backward and I went to high school with most everyone there, but for right now, just right now, it's okay because my brother's here.

I couldn't hack school last year at another college because I was lonely and I failed most everything. I tell everyone it was from the drugs or the alcohol but the truth is I was just lonely and cried all the time and lived in an old house with lots of dust.

This is what they say:

Didn't like it there man? That place is fucking cool, fucking badass town man, why'd you leave man, I mean why'd you come back here?

This is what I say:

Too much, just too much.

And then they say this:

Yeah man I understand that I mean that town does it to the best of them man, gets everybody all fucked up with all that shit they got there, there's so much shit there man, you know I understand that shit really.

And Brett gave up a soccer scholarship upstate. He didn't want to do the summer workout and couldn't make up his mind about anything, and it's lame to be here and we know it, but it's cool and livable for a little while because just a few minutes ago Brett and I decided to leave here next semester. We got the idea a few days ago when we helped a friend move in at Clemson where everything's huge and it's where my grandfather went and where my dad went and after we decided Brett said fuck yeah and I said yeah fuck man.

Both of us.

Gone.

So this party in August is the beginning of the end of our time here.

We leave after Christmas.

THIS PARTY IS just a party with people from all over the town, which is not really a college town even though we have a college. Brett and I aren't in a fraternity but it doesn't matter even though it's a frat party because if there's a party, any party, anyone who sees it, or knows about it, or hears about it comes, because the town's small and there's not much else to do.

The town's named Florence and it's this crumbling place in South Carolina with steel mills and railroad tracks. There's a country club made up of all the old families and the new ones who have money. And even though Brett and I have lived here for three years we don't come from here and our dad's a preacher but he's strange (not like hellfire crazy strange, or standing on a sidewalk holding a Bible up in the air strange, but just strange, like once he melted down the gold caps from his teeth and made them into a cross) and he doesn't have enough money to be in the club and neither does my mother (she's a school nurse and when we get sick she's always the one who tells us we'll be better soon, tells us what pills to eat) but occasionally we get invited to their parties because we know the sons and the daughters, and it's always us just standing there with our cigarettes and the free booze, but we know we aren't like them and we couldn't marry one of the daughters because we don't come from where their future husbands are supposed to.

BRETT'S ONLY THIRTEEN months younger than me but bigger and everyone we meet thinks he's older and I have to say
nah it's me thirteen months and two days.

Me.

Point at my chest.

THAT'S HOW IT always goes. Me measuring up to my brother.
He's good-looking and all the girls swoon when they see him.
Six-one. Dark skin. Brown hair. Broad shoulders. This chiseled
face. My mom and dad say I'm good-looking but it's not the
same as when a girl says it.

For example: My brother and me in our grandparents' driveway playing basketball. I am fifteen. He is fourteen. I am tall for
my age, the only growth spurt I really ever have, full of acne,
awkward, he is shorter and still has that boy look to him. My
first cousin (two years younger, a girl) comes over with one of
her friends. They stand there and look us over, hands on their
hips. My cousin looks over at her friend, says what do you think
about Brett, like she's trying to set her friend up and the friend
says oh he's fine. Gnaws her fingernail. My cousin asks about
me. Weird, the friend says, he's weird. Looks at the ground.

There you go.

And it isn't just the looks. It's everything. Brett is athletic. He
makes all-state in soccer junior and senior years. I quit soccer
when I am twelve. I quit tennis when I am fourteen. I am good
at neither. But mostly it's just the air about him. Like he can
have anything he wants. He just needs to point.

Another example:

Me seventeen. Him sixteen. Me drunk and standing by a fire. Arms crossed. Brett inside the tent, the door zipped. The tent shifting. I'm facing this girl Kathleen across the fire, her face lit orange, and we don't know what to say to each other. Breath fogged. Brett's head from the tent door. Then he's standing. Kathleen's cousin Alice leaving the tent after Brett. Brett smoking. Alice shaking. Both back inside the tent. And I keep shaking, looking over at Kathleen with the words stuck. She tells me I'm boring. I tell her I know. I sleep in the dirt beside the fire. Kathleen goes in the tent with Brett and Alice.

But I know that Brett feels sort of the same way about me. Like he wants the things I've got. He thinks I am creative. I can play guitar and he wants to be able to do that. I start playing guitar after I quit the violin, then the piano, then the trumpet. And he thinks I'm smart. But I'm always thinking fuck smart and creative. I just feel weird. With Brett and me it's like this dual-adoration thing but the truth is I'd give all the stuff he wants for all the stuff I want in a heartbeat.

And this is also Brett and me:

This band we have in high school. Me fifteen. Him fourteen. Brett singing. Me playing guitar. This kid Chris on the drums. This other kid John Michael on bass. The band's name is Lethal Injection. We draw syringes on pieces of paper. Write Lethal on top. Injection on the bottom. Record this song in the room Brett and I share. Use this tape deck. The song is called "Fuck the School and the Administration" and the creative impetus for this song comes from a phrase written in green spray paint on a sidewalk at our high school. The song has three chords, G, C, D, over and over. The words:

(Verse)
Teachers suck.
School sucks.
Food sucks.
Everything sucks.
(Chorus)
Fuck the school (Brett singing this part).
And the administration (Me singing this part).
(Repeat)

We hate everybody then. All the country club fucks. All the football players. This is who we like: ourselves. And we both agree the word cool is used too lightly. There are these cool people out in the world, fictional or otherwise: Holden Caulfield. Axl Rose. Kurt Cobain. The Clash. And that's about it. Who's cool besides these people? we say. Who deserves the word? We look at each other. Nod. Us, we say. You and me. And we know it's true.

AND THERE ON the porch Brett tells me this: we should fuck these two girls. The short one. The shaky one. Me and him. And I can see myself with the shaky one, all sweat and open mouths, and I'm there, right there, me and Brett with these two girls in some smoke-filled apartment.

But then I remember that I can't because I don't do these things. Because when these things happen there's always this part of me that can't talk, this part of me that knows I won't be good at the sex, this part of me that stumbles and shakes around girls. But Brett doesn't shake. He does these things.

And right now my hands are shaking and I say I don't know (look around) and I try and think of an excuse, I'm tired man, long day you know, and that's what comes out, this excuse, this reason I know Brett has heard before. Brett nods yeah but I know he wants this for me more than he wants it for himself, like it's a gift, but for some reason I can't take it or be like him, and I'm nineteen years old and I weigh one hundred thirty-two pounds and my hands shake a lot and I'm always nervous and scared but I don't know why.

WHEN THE GIRLS are gone and I know I'll leave soon, Brett looks me over and says you sure about leaving? and I say yeah, I'm cool, turn eyes to the floor, drag the cigarette and he puts a hand flat on my back and without saying anything else he turns around and then he's gone. Inside the house. All these bodies moving up around him. I stay leaned up against the porch railing alone. The street that runs in front of the house is dark both ways, shrouded by oaks leaning in. The sky is ash.

AND THE VOICE comes soft at my back. Over my shoulder. I am walking down the sidewalk away from the porch to my car. I turn my head and he's there, this face I don't know, all teeth and glowing eyes, one hand laid against the chain-link fence running along my right shoulder. One hand is shoved down into his left pocket. He cocks his head to the side.

So, he says, so man give me a ride right? and I look at him and my head drops, yes, sure, yeah, where you going, up the street, he says, just up the street, hand pointed now, the index finger hooked at the knuckle. And inside I'm shaking my head, telling him no, no ride, sorry gotta be somewhere, but I can't stop myself from saying yes. My head also saying this is a stranger but I think I have seen him here, at this party strolling, sipping a beer, placing a hand on a girl's back, throwing his lit smile into the dark. Or maybe this person is simply someone who needs a ride and I can't say no because I'm afraid to tell people no.

And then the smile is turned around saying I'll be back, let me get my boy, right back, and I'm standing there with my hands in my pockets sweating in the dark heat, pulling the bottom of my shirt up to my forehead, again thinking turn and go, just turn and go, but my feet won't move and before I can breathe again the smile is back saying hey man this is my boy and I'm shaking hands with both of them and their skin is cool and rough and I'm nodding, pulling keys from my pocket. I unlock the door to my car, this maroon Oldsmobile with the streetlights gleaming off the hood. Drop down into the seat and pull the door shut. Fumble with the keys. They shake in my hand like a rattle. The smile is looking down into the car. I lean over across the passenger seat and pull up the silver lock.

INSIDE THE CAR the smile speaks of the school where he goes, says he's leaving tomorrow to go back, and the pussy, he says, ah man the pussy, so much it's everywhere, and I say yeah man I know, even though I don't and we stop at a gas station where the smile gets out and goes inside and through the windows I can see him leaning over the front counter and he's moving his head back and forth smiling. He takes a step back and points at the girl behind the register. Still smiling. She hands him a torn piece of paper. He looks it over and folds it once, shoves it down into his back pocket. I look at the rear-view into the seat behind me and it's a head turned sideways, this silent profile, forearm strung like concrete across the top of the backseat, and when he turns I look down at the radio. The car shifts when he leans toward the front seat, and for a moment, I can feel his breath from behind me. The passenger door opens and the smile's back inside, he says got that number, points at the girl in the gas station. He's throwing candy at the breath in the backseat. He sits down. More candy in his lap.

That way, he says. That way. And the car's moving again. Inside the car the sound of wrappers tearing and being pulled apart.

WE ARE SPEEDING and I can't stop smoking. I'm leaning all the way against my window blowing smoke over the edge trying to think of a way to be done with this ride and all that comes is this: drive and it will end. I'm telling myself this is nothing, no, nothing, but we drive a long way and the street-lights get farther apart.

AND THEN I know that they're leading me nowhere. They want me somewhere dark. I can feel them looking at me, the smile in the passenger seat, his teeth bared in a snarl, the breath in the back, his frozen silence. These bodies around me. These bodies who keep telling me this: not much farther just up the road just up the road and me nodding my head yes yes.

We drive on back roads and the eyes of deer are caught in the headlights. They stand there staring, dark trees at their backs. The road bends sharply and around a curve I want the head-lights to lock a deer in the road so I can't stop, so it will crush the front end of my car.

But then I tell myself again that this is nothing. That it will be done soon, that I will stop the car and the smile and the breath will leave and it will all be over, this ride, this shaking, it will be done.

THE SMILE TUNES the radio. I speed and hope I'll get pulled. When I take another cigarette the smile is looking at me and I see him but I don't turn, he's there smiling, the electronic dial on the radio bleeding blue onto his legs and stomach. Smoke? he says and I say yeah smoke, I smoke, hold the cigarette toward him, shake it a bit, want one? I say and he laughs, says nah I mean smoke, you know like real smoke? and it takes me a minute to get it and then I'm going nah I mean I do (want to sound cool) but I can't right now I mean I shouldn't my ma's got the car in the morning and she doesn't like that stuff wish I could you know but I can't sorry sorry, the smile says you know 'cause we wanted to smoke some with you (points to the back) and again I'm saying wish I could wish we could (lying) I mean that would be cool I like to smoke I mean I do it often I mean all the time as much as I can yeah love to smoke. It's cool the smile says and I take another pull from the ciga-rette, pinch it between my thumb and middle finger, flick it out the window, it flies, burns like a bottle rocket on the pavement behind us.

THE FACTS:

A dirt road.

Parked car.

Streetlights peeling back the dark.

My right hand on the drive stick.

Head turned to the smile.

His teeth like white coals.

So here, I say. Yeah. Take care.

Nod. Look to my right and the moon is the blade of an ax.

I take my eyes from it, turn toward the smile. I smile back.

And the forearm comes from behind me, fills the space be-tween my chin and breastbone. I can feel my neck bend and cave, my Adam's apple cracking and the light shrinks around me. The smile next to me. It's motionless, still as the moon.

I blink once.

Twice and my mouth is sucking air that won't come.

Breath wet on my cheek.

My head goes black.

MY MOUTH FULL of dirt. The air comes back as quickly as it left, fills me, pulses. I'm on the ground with feet beside my face, with feet landing on my ribs. Beneath my car I can see the field and the dry soybeans hunched like gimps. I put my arms and hands around my head and then I'm raised beneath the arms, lifted like a doll. I stagger and can't stand up. The breath holds me around the chest. The smile is in front of me, teeth clenched, puts fists into my eyes, my mouth. Tears a chain from my neck.

Dangles it in front of me. And then he's in my back pockets. Pulls the wallet. Dumps everything he doesn't want into the dirt. Next: the keys. Jammed into the smile's pocket.

This is what I say:

Credit card. Code. Four. Four. Four. Four.

Please. Leave me here.

This is what the smile says:

Not enough.

We want it all.

I'm crying.

The smile: stop fucking crying.

The breath behind me: snap your neck.

The forearm around my neck tightening. I'm yanking down, digging nails into the skin. It doesn't move. And the fists come again into my face. My mouth full of blood. Swallow it. I can feel my heart in my temples. The smile bobs, looks as if he loves me and there is no sound, the locusts have stopped, the street lamps have quit humming. But there is this: my ears ringing, air trying to enter me and the breath behind me, lips wet against my ear, he's saying this over and over: go to sleep go to sleep.

AND THE TRUNK open, the light from inside falling onto the smile's chest. Behind him the field black, the treeline black and shrouded with the faint white of the moon touching the heads of pine. The smile throwing a broken golf club into the field. Throwing my book bag. The books spill out, the pages flutter like wings. Everything dirt and dust. I'm watching from the ground, head straight down, eyes raised, my mouth open in the dirt, all blood and spit and clay, arms laid straight at my side, the breath his foot on my back grinding my spine down with his heel. He drags it gently up my back, lets it rest on my neck, mashes the toe into my skull, holds it there and I can feel my nose breaking. The breath takes his foot away, the smile down next to my face on his knees, palms laid flat in the dust. I don't want to look at him but I turn my eyes up anyway. His eyes level with mine, he smiles and smiles.

THEN THE SMILE'S feet in my mouth. The breath beside me, his feet in my stomach. Picking me up beneath the arms again and I'm limp, my eyes clouded and the blood foaming on my lips, running down my chin. It's falling down my chest and there's so much blood I'm drinking it, the smile in front of me now, his warm breath on my cheek, he's looking me square in the face. Wake up, he says, slaps my face with his rough cold hand, walk motherfucker, walk, he says, move your fucking legs and they're moving. The breath is carrying me, legs all wobble and shake, I'm dragging my shoes leaving lines in the dust toward the trunk. It's open for me. I crawl in and lay down, curled like a baby holding my legs up to my chest and my eyes move up, the light from inside the trunk on the smile's chest, on the breath's chest, they're both standing there and the breath sees my eyes on them and says don't fucking look keep your fucking eyes closed you want to breathe huh? you want to breathe? Then the trunk snaps shut and the light is gone.

INSIDE THE TRUNK of a car the fetal position is most comfortable.

Here is what you do:

Draw knees up against the chest.

Wrap bicep and forearm over the shins.

Adjust to the rise of wheel over stone.

Lie silent.

Breathe deliberately.

Know this:

All that is real is the shrunken dark.

Smell of blood and sweat.

Of dirt and smoke.

Sound of bass and blunt laugh.

Open my eyes and it is all dark and I squint to make them work to make them see but they will not. I'm lying on my side with my knees pulled up against my chest. I push one hand into the dark. I trace the steel ribs of the trunk's frame behind me and I know that if I'm left in the trunk I can push the backseat's cushions, wedge myself through the ribs. I learned this once when I locked the keys in my trunk. A friend said you know you can pull the cushions out right? crawl through the frame? and I shook my head no I did not know that, but now I do, here in all this dark I know. I run my hands through the space around my legs, my chest, try to find something to hold, something to use. There's a plastic pen near my face and I take it, trembling, and I love the smile for leaving it for me and for a moment I see myself rising from the trunk when the door is opened, rising like mist, this pen held like a knife, I'm tearing the smile's throat, I'm jamming the pen into the breath's neck, we're covered in blood and blue ink, me holding a foot above the breath's neck and then I'm stomping the pen down, nailing him to the dirt and the smile is holding his throat, gasping, fingers painted red and blue. But then I know that I will suffocate here, that I will be left to bake. I pull the ink shaft from the top of the pen and what's left is a hollow plastic tube and I'm thinking that this hollowed-out pen is the only thing that will let me breathe, and then I have the pen clutched between my lips, jamming it into a space where I think there might be air and I'm sucking and the pen drops to the floor and rolls away and I put my whole mouth over the space like it's a nipple.

I FEEL THE road beneath me change from gravel to asphalt. The tires smooth. I find the hollowed pen and hold it with a baby's grip, pull knees tight to my chest and let my eyes close.

The tires stop. A car door opens then shuts. The car moves again.

THE MOON HANGING over the smile's shoulder. He is shrouded in dark, holding the trunk open. The breath beside him, dark arms at his side. They are shadow. The light inside the trunk burns my eyes. I hold my hand above them and blink hard. Squint. The breath's fist in my head, told you not to look boy he says, put your fucking eyes down, and I drop my eyes, cover my head with forearms. The smile says get up don't look get up and don't fucking look and I've got my head down, moving my legs over the edge of the trunk, the breath pulling me out. And then I'm on my knees in the dust looking up again. Don't look the breath says, his foot in my ribs and I want to say I can't see you I can't you are nothing. I want to say leave me here just leave me, take the car, just leave, I won't tell. And then my lips are stuttering the words, I won't tell swear to God I can't see you I can't just leave me here. The smile says nah too late, tells me to get up and I can't, my legs won't move, the breath drags me by the back of my shirt, my knees against the dirt and stone. Pushes me down in front of the car. Headlights against my back. Presses my face into stones on the road. They cut into my cheek and forehead. He leaves his hand on the back of my head for a moment, holds me there, says put your hands behind your head don't look up don't look up you want to breathe huh? yeah you do don't move your fucking head and his hand is gone and I leave my head there pressed into the rocks as stiffly as when the breath's hand held it and my eyes are open not looking back into the light but sideways across the stones, over a ditch into the tangled woods, and I want to run, I want to stand up and leave but I am locked here and I know that I will die soon.

But then I am calm. It spreads over me like rain. I concentrate on the outline of tree pressing against tree, dust moving through the headlights that fall over me and I am waiting for a gun's steel to press against the back of my skull, I am waiting for the click of the trigger, I am waiting for the soft kiss, I am waiting for my eyes to go black.

And when the car starts I am waiting for the tires to break my skull, to crush my ribs. I brace and tense my muscles. Eyes closed. The car whines backward. The sound gets smaller until it is nothing, until nothing is left but the moan of insects.

I RUN UNTIL my heart explodes and my legs crumble and I fall into tall grass to my right, fall into a ditch. The grass swallows me whole. I sink, dig my hands into the mud, curl myself like a fist, wait for the sound of one engine to return, the sound of car doors opening, clicking shut, the smile and the breath panting, snapping tree limbs, parting the grass inside the ditch, dropping their hot eyes down onto me. And inside the grass and mud my head goes black.

WATER IN MY mouth wakes me. I rise to my knees and cough there in the grass and the blood from my mouth mixes with the mud and standing water. Painted red and brown I am a ghost. My face, my arms, my clothes are covered. Inside the ditch tall grass wraps my shoulders, my arms, my neck. I am standing in water up to my ankles. My feet sink into mud. Over the edge, through grass, I can see the road strewn with granite. The moon lights the granite's sharp faces and they shine, sparkle like a long bed of jewels reaching out in both directions into black. Behind me the woods are thick and moving.

I WILL NOT take the road. I crawl out of the ditch and run to the woods at my back, hunch down beneath the pines. I can hear every movement, every branch snapping, every break of dried leaves and for the first time I think of my brother sleeping beside the girl with the torn shirt and muscled legs, her breath on his chest, his mouth open toward the ceiling, and for the first time I know that I have to move through these woods, that I have to move toward him and I see my mother and father sleeping and my bed lying empty and still. But my legs won't move so I stay bent over staring out into the dark.

I move away from the road, into the woods. I push branches aside, my feet tangled in thorns and the teeth tear into my shins and calves when I pull each leg up and the roots hold firm and the teeth tear deeper and the pain is hot and the blood is filling my shoes again but I raise each leg and jerk until the teeth are lodged in my shins and calves but the roots give and I'm trailing them behind me.

The woods open into a field, and in the black I see a set of eyes cast silver from the moon. I'm taking steps, walking toward the burning eyes. I drop to my knees and stare, the eyes shake, trail silver streaks in the dark. When I'm still, I can hear my heart pulsing. Behind and below the eyes there's burnt dull red, a muzzle white and dark gray. It's this fox stepping toward me, placing its feet cautiously into the dirt. And we're both bent down staring at each other and the fox just looks straight at me with the white eyes and the neck bent to smell the soil and for a long time I just stare and the fox just stares. The fox turns the dirt with his front feet. Lies down and breathes and I can see the outline of rib. I am stomach down. Forearms beneath my chin.

And then I know that I can talk to this fox.

I ask the fox for a name.

No name, the fox says, just fox or red fox or red, whatever, nothing like you'd think, you know?

The mouth never moves, the voice comes through the eyes.

Boy or girl? I say.

That doesn't matter now does it? the fox says. I'm a fox and you're talking to a fox here in this field. Does it really matter if I'm a boy or a girl?

No, you're right, I say, I was just curious and then I think about asking the fox how to leave, how to get out, and then I do.

Leave? the fox says. Why would you want to leave? This is a great field. You know how fast I am, right?

No, I don't know how fast you are.

Yeah, very fast, I'm very fast. You should see it, these dogs, they think they can get me with their noses and yelps, those yelps like something dying, but they're dumb, I mean come on, what do they think, they can come in here where I live, on my place, my dirt, this is mine, you know I own it?

I nod.

They run around yelping and think I'll be scared. You wanna see my teeth?

Yeah. The fox turns the black lips up, these small sharp white teeth lining the dark gums, drops the lips back down.

Nice huh? the fox says.

Yeah.

Go on, the fox says, let me see your teeth and I pull my gums up. Those aren't too bad, the fox says. Wanna hear my growl?

Yeah, I say. The fox growls this low grumbling sound that comes deep from the throat. Yeah, I say, that's nice a good growl and the teeth, those are quite impressive.

I know, the fox says, I come from a long line of good teeth and growls. You got a good growl, I mean one you use for special occasions?

No, I say, I don't really have a growl at all.

Of course you do, the fox says, try.

Okay, I say. I start to bring the growl from deep inside my chest.

Not bad, not bad, the fox says. That's not a bad growl you've got there, keep practicing, you don't just get a great growl overnight. Some of us are born with them and it doesn't take much but even when you're born with one you can always push it further, you can always make it better.

This place, I say, I need to leave and the fox just looks at me. Really? the fox says.

I have to, I say, and then I push up with my hands and settle on my knees. I raise one leg, place a foot out in front and the fox rises, tenses, jerks and is gone.

AT THE BACK of the field, I duck into woods again, and inside a clearing where the trees part, pine straw like dark hair on the ground, there's a bulldozer, there alone, trees standing like columns at its back. Yellow. Black script. Says Caterpillar along the sides. Treads filled with dirt. Long arm raised, bent toward the front glass of the driver's seat. The shovel at the end of the arm curled, soil spilling through its fingers. I stare for a long time at the machine and then I climb the sides and open the glass door. Drop into the seat. Run my hands beneath the steering wheel looking for keys. I find them in the ignition. A hat that says Peterbilt beside the gearshift. I bend down and take the hat. Torn. Sweat-stained. Pull it down onto my head. A red cigarette pack on the floorboard. Pall Mall. I bend to get the crumpled pack, bring it close to my face but it's empty. I throw it back onto the floorboard and look straight ahead at the

fogged glass, the woods tangled and thick, the moon pale white
over everything and now I know that I will drive the bulldozer
from the woods, that I will plow trees and shacks aside, that I
will drop the long arm down and pull trees, roots dripping
with dirt, I will lay them down and carve a path with the engine rattling and the exhaust rising in tufts behind me and I will
fall out with the blood and the dirt caked and the thorns choking my legs and there will be a crowd gathered and they will
stare like I am a ghost, like I have risen from the soil, like I am
Lazarus stumbling from the grave with the dirt falling from his
mouth. I will ride out and the crowd gathered will shake their
heads, he was dead, they'll say, he was dead, and I will look
them over and not say anything, I will show them my face,
I will show them my torn body, I will leave them with the
memory of my blood.

But the engine will not start. I turn the keys, fumble with the
gears and then I'm beating the glass in front of me, slamming
my fists against the fogged pane, I'm screaming against these
woods and this darkness that will not let me go.

WHEN I COME out of the woods, it's the same as when I went
into them. Just after the trees end, there's a ditch beside a road.
I drop into the tall grass. Look out over the edge. The same
stones laid bare and knotted close. I know it's part of the same
road, that it's the same stones that tore my face, that it's the
only road that I'll find because covered in dirt and blood and
stumbling through field and woods I found nothing.

I CHOOSE A direction. Move to my right.

I stay in the ditch beside the road and when headlights appear behind me I fall back down into the grass.

But the car is white. It moves by slowly, swerves a bit farther down the road. And my body will not move. I push hair away from my face and wait until everything is quiet.

ON THE WINDOWPANE the image of the television colored blue and red and white and green and black and pink in bars from when the station went quiet. I press my face against the glass. Inside the television lights a pale face and bare stomach, a gleaming scalp, one hand dropped over the side of a chair, a cigarette smoldering in an ashtray that sits on the lap, a bottle and glass on the table beside the chair. The bald man does not stir when I put my fist against the window. I begin softly but then I'm pounding the glass. He does not move, he only breathes and lets the color light his face.

I open the driver's side door of a car in the yard and grasp for keys in the ignition. Beneath seats, under sun visors. I blow the horn. I wait and when nothing happens I get out of the car because I know I can't stay in one place for too long.

I move along the road, stay near the woods, and when I see a light from a house ahead of me, I run toward it.

I FALL DOWN in the front yard of a small house. One light burning on the porch. Insects like sparks around the light. I take the steps and lay my fists against the red wooden door and I hear nothing, and I bring my fists down again, say please this is my last chance please, press my face against the cold wood and then there is the shuffling of feet across a floor and the door pulling open, the chain attached, the light overhead burning a woman's eyes all bleary and cracked around the edges.

What? she says. Who are you? And then she sees my blood, looks me up and down and then I'm mumbling *please*.

Hold on, she says, just wait. The door shutting, lock clicking, feet shuffling over the floor again and then a man with the same red cracked eyes.

What do you want? he says.

Please, I say, hold a hand to my face and for the first time I see my hands clearly, dried red and brown, soil beneath my fingernails and the cuts standing open like smiles. Please, I say and the man opens the door a bit more. He's standing there in blue boxer shorts, a white T-shirt, his hair standing up on top, pressed down on the sides, he puts a hand softly against his wife's chest, he's still looking at me, he nudges her back and she's there in her nightgown with the arms crossed and he comes out onto the porch, shuts the screen door behind him.

Son, he says, what is this, son?

Stole my car, I say, it was them. Point down the road from where I came.

Who? he says.

Them, I say, I don't know, it was them. He looks me over and his eyes squint and he sits me down on a porch swing and then I'm crying. Thank you, I say, and he puts a hand on my shoulder.

I'll get a phone, he says and then he's back in the house letting the door fall quietly shut behind him and I'm sitting there in the swing with my arms drawn across my chest and my face turned down to the porch and the light at my feet.

THE WOMAN SITS beside me on the porch swing. The chains whine.

Police are on the way, son, she says. Your dad.

I nod. She's smoking a cigarette and I want one.

Can I have a cigarette? I say.

It'll hurt, she says. I nod, she shakes one from the pack (Winstons), I raise my hand but she pushes it back down, takes the cigarette between her teeth, brings the lighter up, the flame red against her face. She pulls, lets the smoke bleed from her mouth, takes the cigarette, turns it around and presses the filter softly against my lips.

The smoke traces my cheeks, runs into my eyes. The smoke rises up into the porch lights, hovers there and is gone.

MY FATHER'S HAND on my shoulder. Standing above me. His face clenched. I look up at him, all right, I say, I'm fine, and then I laugh to show him I'm fine but he knows I'm not. He knows I won't be fine and then Brett sits beside me on the porch swing, his hair all mashed flat and his mouth tightens and he is sobbing and touching my face, his hands against my cheeks, on my neck. It's all right, I say, I'm okay, fine really, but he shakes his head back and forth and he keeps crying and he says no no over and over.

TWO POLICEMEN ASK me questions.

How many men?

Two, I say.

What did they look like?

Shadows, I say.

Did you know the men?

No, I say.

Why did you give them a ride?

Don't know, I say.

Where is your car?

They took it, I say, and then I tell them about the bulldozer and I tell them it was the smile, it was the breath but they are ghosts, you won't catch them I say, they're shadows I say, poof I say, fucking gone man, you can't even see them I say, and they nod their heads yes oh yes and then I'm laughing and then I say fuck man you guys don't even know you can't fucking know you can't fucking know and I laugh I laugh and Brett is leaning against the porch railing with his arms crossed over his chest and he doesn't say anything and my father is sitting beside me and he doesn't say anything.

I LEAVE WITH my father and brother and inside the car my father is staring straight ahead. Brett's in the passenger seat watching fields pass. I'm also watching fields pass. Behind those fields, over the treeline, the sun rising bloodred.

INSIDE THE EMERGENCY room I'm the only patient. The walls yellow. The floor polished and white.

The doctor makes me open my mouth. Shines a light into my throat. Takes his fingertips and touches my throat.

This hurt? he says. I nod.

It all hurts, I say and then he's shining a light into my eyes and after he's done he says nothing's broken, that's good, no concussion, just some cuts and bruises and then he's swabbing my face with a cotton ball and I wince. He touches my lips with the cotton ball and then he's at my arm drawing blood and I'm clenching a fist and watching my blood fill a glass tube dark like a bruise.

Carbon monoxide, he says, we have to check to see if you were poisoned and I nod my head and he seals the blood, wipes my forearm, stands and turns on his heels to go.

No poisoning, the doctor says, after he's been gone awhile. Beats his thumbs against the clipboard he's holding. You're good as far as that goes but keep those cuts clean, that one on your face, watch it close, it was really dirty when you came in.

I nod.

Okay, I say. I will.

BRETT SITTING IN the waiting room. Chin against his fist. A poster that says Get Your Flu Shot at his back. He stands when he sees my father and me coming toward him. My father tells him I'm not poisoned and he nods, yeah, good, he says and when we go outside the air is damp and hot and it's early but the world is already burning.

WHEN I GET home my mother is waiting on our couch. My youngest brother Matthew is asleep in his room. She stands up and her face tightens when she sees me and she doesn't say anything, she leans close against me and puts her hands on the back of my head. Keeps them there for a long time.

It's okay, Mom, I say and she swallows, doesn't say anything, holds her hands on the back of my head and then she leads me back to my room. She sits me down on the bed. She leans down to my feet, unties my shoes and pulls them off. The bloody socks. My mother gives me a clean T-shirt and sweatpants. I take off my shirt and jeans and put them on. I lay down and my mother hands me a glass of water. A pink pill. She's a nurse so I don't ask what it is. I swallow the pill and my mother draws the sheets up. Looks at my neck, runs her hands along the bruises there. Sleep, she says, it's all right. You'll be fine. You'll feel better. Closes my eyes with the tips of her fingers.

I WAKE AND go into the bathroom. Lay hands flat on the sides of the sink. I look in the mirror.

Around my neck the handprints wrapped like barbed wire.

Face swollen bloodred.

The dried blood, the dirt.

Near my eye a tear like a birthmark.

Eyes blank.

In the glass behind me I see my mother's face. Arms crossed over her chest. I come out. She hands me another pink pill. I swallow it.

BRETT'S FACE OVER my bed. He cries. I hold my hand up and take his and then I can't hold my eyes open anymore, it's okay, he says, it's okay, close your eyes.

MY FATHER COMES in and sits down at the foot of my bed. Tells me that he got a knife and rode around for three hours.

Looking for them, he says. Cut their throats. I tell him that was stupid.

Wanted to kill them, he says. Was going to kill them.

I nod.

You won't find them, I say. You can't.

My father tells me my mother is asleep. She doesn't understand, he says. It's hard for her to figure it out. I nod. He puts a hand on top of my right shin and leaves it there for a moment.

And even now I know she can't ever know this thing, that it's something she simply can't do. She can't even watch movies because they stay in her head so long.

BRETT COMES IN after my father leaves. Sits at the foot. Tells me my friend Tom got his gun and went looking for them too, said he was going to kill those fuckers. I tell Brett that was stupid. He nods.

I know, he says.

You can't find them, I say. Tom can't. Guns won't work. Nothing would work. They're not even real, they're shadows.

He nods yeah, like he understands but I know he doesn't, he doesn't know, he can't know. They're not men, I say, they're ghosts and he's nodding again.

I know, he says, I know. I shake my head.

No, you don't, I say, no, you don't.

2

A N ELEVATOR DOOR opening. My father stepping in first. Turning to look at me, holding his hand out. I take it and step inside. We're at the district attorney's office in another town because I was beaten in another county. I sit with my father on a brown leather couch, and lining the walls are pictures of old men with white hair and they're all in robes. A woman comes in behind us, I feel her pass by me, the air shifts and she smells like flowers and then she's behind her desk with her elbows propped and her fingers laced together. She looks at me and smiles and I smile back even though it hurts and her hair catches the light coming through the blinds and she's wearing a navy blue suit.

You've been through a lot I know, she says.

I nod.

So what I'm here to do is to punish those who did this to you, okay? she says and I nod again.

Yes, I say, the bones of her face sharp in the light.

So I'm going to ask you some questions, she says, and I know it might be hard to answer but if you could do your best that's all I ask.

Sure, I say, okay, I'll do my best, and I say it because I love her now because she is smiling at me.

GRAVEL CRUNCHING BENEATH tires in the police station parking lot. I am here to answer questions about what happened. The sun dropping behind the station, behind the treeline, and the light bleeds red over everything, streaming through the windshield and landing on my chest. It's warm and I close my eyes and let it stay there pressed like an open palm.

My father's hand on my shoulder.

Time to go, he says.

I nod. Open the door and drop my feet down into the gravel. The light shrinking. I follow my father across the parking lot.

AN OFFICER TAKES me to a room past the waiting area, and my father has to stay behind. The officer sits me down at a long table in the center of a room with desks where other officers are typing. Some talking on the phone. I hear papers shuffle. The officer taps me on the left shoulder. I jump.

Sorry, he says. I turn and he's there sitting beside me with a yellow legal pad and a pencil. Pushes the square glasses up his nose, he leans in toward me, breath hot against my face. I turn my head down to the table.

Write, he says, I want you to write it down just like it happened.

Sure, I say. He slides the pencil and the pad in front of me and I take the pencil, clutch it tight between my fingers, run one hand over the paper and the officer leaves and the pencil starts to move and I can't stop. I'm writing about teeth and growls and foxes and smiles and breaths and I know it makes no sense but I know at the same time that every word is true.

THE OFFICER TAKES the pad from me. Hands me a book.

Look at some pictures, he says, just flip through these and tell me if you recognize any.

Shoves blank white paper toward me.

You write down the numbers, he says. Opens the book in the middle, points to a picture. See? he says, like this. Points to the numbers below a picture of a white man with a blond crew cut. Okay, he says, you got that? Just write down numbers, okay? I nod.

Yeah, I say, I can do that.

Start at the beginning, he says.

Right, I say and he turns the book to the first page, stands up and leaves. I can't make any sense of the pictures. I don't write anything.

WHAT I WANT to know is this. How come a nice-looking boy like you picks up two guys you don't even know and gives them a ride? A long ride. To the middle of nowhere.

I've been moved. I'm sitting at another table in a room separated from the big office. I hate these cops and I want to be left alone. There's a mirror behind me. The officer with the shaved head sits in front of me. Asking me questions. Now the officer with the brown mustache stands behind him.

Who said I was nice-looking?

My eyes down on the table.

I did.

Oh.

So. Clear it up.

I told you already. I wrote it down.

He holds up a yellow legal pad with my scribbles. This? This is junk. I can't understand this. You wrote about foxes. You didn't write any numbers from the pictures.

He throws the pad down on the table.

It's true, I say. It's all I know.

It doesn't make any sense, son, I know you were out of your head but it doesn't make any sense, it doesn't mean anything to us.

That's what I remember. I can't get at anything else.

I'll tell you what I think happened. He leans toward me. I think you wanted drugs. You were trying to buy drugs. I look at him and shake my head.

I don't do drugs. (Lying.)

Yes, you do.

No, I don't.

You do do drugs. We know you do drugs.

You don't.

We do.

No.

Yes.

No.

Listen, son, we already got one, he's right back there, says
you wanted drugs from him, says he knew you already.

Right back there?

I point toward the mirror behind me.

Yeah. Right back there. Says he knew you good.

I shake my head.

You can't catch them. Him. Them.

We did, he's right back there, you want me to bring that boy
in here so you can look him in the face?

I look up at him.

He doesn't have a face. I say it softly.

What? The officer leans closer. What? His face red.

I said he doesn't have a face.

Both officers look at me like I'm crazy but I know I'm not.

I MISS A week of school. The cuts on my face heal into shiny
red patches. The bruises turn dull and gray. My lips are only a
little swollen. My mother says look you're better already, and
she knows I'm not, but I know she can't deal with this thing, so
all she knows to do is give me pills and Neosporin and tell me
I'll be better. Nobody says anything and I like it that way. My
teachers understand the absence. Make concessions. But even
when I'm there at school, sitting in Cultural Geography or Po-
litical Science I'm not really there. I'm dreaming. I'm shaking.
The smile and the breath everywhere. In breezeways. Walking
down halls. Sitting at the back of classrooms. I have to go into
bathrooms, pull the stall doors shut and slap my face until my
ears ring.

I'M IN THE car with the brown mustache speeding past fields through dark. He's got both hands on top of the steering wheel. We're trying to find the road where the smile and the breath left me. The road I wrote about on the yellow legal pad. We have to look in the dark because it's the only time the brown mustache can go. He looks over at me with my hands in my lap and my head down.

Need you to look, son, he says and I nod, raise my head to the window, to the fields, the treeline, the lumped soil and bent soybean.

I am, I say, and I am looking but I don't recognize anything, just this blackness and the moon standing over everything.

I ASK THE officer for a cigarette. He looks over at me, his face dark.

Why do you think I smoke? he says.

Because, I say, I can smell it in here and he raises a hand to his shirt pocket and pulls a crumpled pack from it just like I knew he would. He holds the pack toward me and I take it, shake out a smoke and then he hands me a lighter and I hold the flame up inside the dark, it lights my arms, my chest. I blow the smoke out the window and hand the lighter back and he takes a smoke and lights it and I wonder why he hasn't smoked yet, but I don't ask. We just sit there driving and smoking and this is all there is.

UNTIL THE CAR slows and he says that look familiar?

It's an old logging road, he says. Don't use it much anymore but that house you found it's not too far from here. This was the only place I could think of.

The car's stopped at the head of a road with the headlights lighting both sides, the pine, the tall grass leaning over the lip of the ditch. The brown mustache gets out and stands with one forearm draped over the edge of the open door.

Get out, son, he says, I need you to look.

Okay, I say. Open the door, and beneath my feet through my shoes I feel the same heads of granite push into my soles and I don't even have to look anymore. I get back in the car and shut the door, the officer gets back in and shuts the door.

Son, he says, what's wrong?

This is it, I say, I know it.

How? You didn't even look.

I just know I could feel it through my feet those stones those are the same it's like a hand you know every time you take this hand you've held you know it?

I'M LOOKING DOWN into the floorboard, the torn coffee cups, a hammer with tape on the head, I keep my eyes there. We can leave now, I say, can we leave now? and I'm rocking back and forth in my seat, hands against the dashboard, my heart clenching, the officer looks over at me, puts the car in reverse and backs up, the granite beneath the tires giving way, and then we're back on the asphalt, we drive away and I rock in my seat, I laugh and the officer turns the radio up loud this country station Hank Williams I'm a long gone daddy I don't need you anymore he says.

Hank the senior, the officer says, he was one of the good ones.

Yeah yeah you know how he died, right? I say. The officer turns the song down.

Yeah, he says, he was a drunk.

No actually that's wrong well he was a drunk but that's not how he died see he had some problems, back or something, I don't know, but it was chronic, like it hurt all the time, so he had this doctor who gave him pills for the pain, and he got hooked and ate too many pills with whiskey one night in Louisiana I think, and the band was Hank Williams and the Drifting Cowboys, something like that, and Hank he died in the backseat of a car driving somewhere, and the doctor he turned out to be a fake doctor.

The brown mustache just looks over at me.

That so? he says, I didn't know all that how do you know all that?

I have all this useless information in my head, I say, you know just banging around up there all this stuff and sometimes I just have to spit it out even if it's not exactly right you know the stuff about Hank that might not be exactly right.

The officer nods.

Well, he says, it sounds like a good story to me. He breathes out, scratches his shoulder.

We drive back to the police station. I can see my father's car in the parking lot. I can see him sitting there resting his arms against the steering wheel.

WHEN WE WENT to get him he took off, he says. Playing basketball with all these boys he saw the car and shot off. Right to the woods. But we couldn't catch him. I'd be willing to guess that he's left the state.

The brown mustache is saying all this to me, a week after we drove around looking for the road. I'm sitting in his office in a chair directly facing his desk, my hands are in my lap and I'm slouched over. The light inside is bright and plain. There's a framed picture on his desk of a yellow Lab.

We picked up the other one a few days ago, he says. He's already said they did it. Told us everything.

I nod.

Okay, I say.

Part of a car theft ring. They found your car a few counties up. They tore it up though. The boys who had it told us about these two. And when we picked up the first one he told us everything, where to find the other one.

I want to ask why they wanted to know about drugs, why they insisted, why they didn't believe me, even after they saw my face and I know that both the brown mustache and the officer with the shaved head were lying, that there was no boy behind the window. I want to ask why he's making no attempt to cover his lie, it is so plain there floating between us but he's just sitting there, and I'm tired and want to be done with this.

We just need you to look at their pictures, he says. Just their pictures. Even though we don't have the other one we've got his picture. Both of those boys have been in trouble before. We have to put a few others in, you know, but only a few. He leans over his desk.

He says I want you to pay attention now, son, when I show you these.

I don't say anything.

All right? he says.

Okay, I say.

He pushes a sheet across the desk toward me. I lean over to the desk, put my elbows on it and look. And it's six men, the top row, the first two across white, the third black, and the bottom row it's one white man, the last two black and then I see these faces, the bottom row, the last two, and I know these faces, know the cheekbones, the mouths, the eyes and I can't stop looking at them, I'm staring down. The officer reaches over and touches my forearm and I jerk it back, I'm still looking.

Son, do you see them? he says and I can't say anything but I place my hand over the two faces, run spread fingers across the pictures and then I hold my palm there flat and the officer takes the picture sheet from beneath my hand, pulls it toward his chest and then he stands up.

THIS IS WHAT happens: The breath pleads guilty. The smile fled. I don't testify. He gets seventy-five years. These are the charges: Grand theft auto. Kidnapping. Strong-arm assault and battery. They're gone but they aren't gone. I can see them everywhere. The smile and the breath are out walking. Always just at my back.

3

WHEN LEAH PICKS me up I'm applying paste to my mouth.

My mother calls me from the hall.

I'm leaned over the sink toward the mirror and I'm sticking my tongue out, dabbing it with tissue, laying the paste all over. My mother has taped Bible verses all over the edge of the mirror because she thinks it will help but it doesn't. The verses written on index cards in her sharp handwriting. Though I walk through the valley of the shadow of death I will fear no evil. Do not fear the reproach of men or be terrified by their insults for the moth will eat them up like a garment.

I have ulcers all over. My tongue, my cheeks, my lips, my throat, like coals in my mouth. The doctor says it's from the stress and from biting my tongue when I got beat up, from having my teeth mashed into my lips. It hurts to breathe, to talk, to swallow. It doesn't hurt so much with the paste, but I can't really open my mouth that wide because then you'd see all the white paste and all the sores. I have antibiotics, because it's like an infection and the doctor says that these ulcers will go away soon.

IN THE HALL between my bedroom and the den there's a picture of Brett and me, we're very small sitting together on a stump surrounded by brown leaves. Brett wearing a tan sweater with a plaid number three on it. His pants are plaid. Hair long and curled on the sides. I'm wearing a red sweater with patches on the white chest band, they're all different colors and supposed to resemble octopi or urchins but really they just look like blobs with eyes. My hair is a bit darker but also curled at the bottom. My pants are navy and I am also smiling. Brett is holding my hand.

In the den my mother and father are sitting on the couch and my father's asking Leah about her parents and Leah says oh they're fine, good, and my parents nod their heads. My youngest brother Matthew comes through the den and my mother says where are you going? and he barely looks up, says out, going out, and he nods at Leah and she nods back, and he takes his keys from a bowl on the television and opens the door.

Leah's standing next to the fireplace and she's got this big smile. Above the fireplace is a portrait of me. My mother had it done when I was a senior and I hate it being there in the den where everyone always sees it because I look goofy with my pleated olive pants, my navy sweater with a blue oxford beneath it. Brett's senior picture is in the hallway and no one sees it like they see mine. There are pictures of Brett and me together everywhere. As babies. As kids. Slumped as teenagers.

Leah is my friend Tom's little sister but he doesn't care that I like her, he says he'd just as soon it be me than some bastard. I say so we should go, right, and look at Leah, hope she can't see in my mouth, and she nods, says yeah, we don't want to miss the game.

IT'S HOMECOMING AT my old high school but it feels strange not only because I am old and shouldn't be going to the football game but because I know everyone knows about me, because everyone looks at me strange, and the whole time I stay close to Leah there in the bleachers with all these people around us. Leah shines beneath the field lights, she glows, and when the wind comes off the field it brings the smell of torn grass, of sweat, of blood. Leah turns her head and I put my face in her hair and she smells like the first light that ever was.

After the game we go to this party, with all these people I know, some I graduated with that are still hanging around, some that are still in high school. It's at a guy's house whose name I don't know, in a subdivision, all manicured lawns and sprinkler systems. And if I could I'd hold Leah's hand the whole time. I wouldn't talk to anyone.

BUT AS SOON as we walk inside I lose her. I can't find her and my heart starts beating, it's in my ears, in my neck and I can't be inside anymore so I don't look at anyone, push my way toward the door, walk down the front steps and out into the yard.

CARS MASHED AGAINST one another. I find Leah's Explorer and sit on the bumper where I think no one will be and while I'm sitting there I light a smoke, blow it up into the hanging leaves still green even though it's close to fall. I look over to my right, a small Honda, the windows dark, the spark of a lighter going off inside. And it opens, smoke spilling out, four boys dropping their legs onto the ground. They walk toward me and in the dark I can't make out faces just outlines, one very tall the others about my height. The tall one calls my name, Brad he says, I hold up one hand, yeah I say, and this boy comes out of shadow. He sits down next to me on the bumper. The others stand. He holds out his hand. I give him mine and then I give it to the rest of them. Danny is the kid on the bumper next to me. He's a big (six-four, two forty-five) eighteen-year-old who works as a carpenter for his dad. There are two other kids standing around me whose names I can't remember. Another kid named Adam. I look over at Danny.

Damn, he says, fucking good smoke.

I nod. Raise my eyebrows.

Oh, yeah? I say.

He coughs. Adam coughs. The others cough.

Yeah, you want? he says. Pats a bulging pocket.

Nah, I say.

Too bad it's good good good, he says.

It's cool, I say.

Okay, he says and then he says just like I knew he would because it is all anyone ever says to me anymore, he says so I heard you got into some shit.

Yeah, I say.

All these boys standing around me making me shake.

Why didn't you just fucking beat the shit out of them? Danny says.

Couldn't really, I say, they were too big and then Danny stands, pulls his sleeve up.

See this? he says, points to his arm, a tattoo of an eagle with a lightning bolt in its beak. I'm going into the marines, he says.

Yeah, cool, I say and he keeps his sleeve up, keeps looking down at his arm, turns to Adam.

You think this is good, right? he says and Adam says fuck yeah. Leah comes around the left side of her car. Sits down beside me. Danny shows her his tattoo.

Yeah, she says, that's really cool and I know she's being sarcastic but he believes it. He flexes the bicep. Pats it. Lets his arm down.

So, he says, just talking to your boy here, asking him how he let two people steal his car and beat the shit out of him.

I have my head down, I drop my smoke on the ground, stab it out with my foot. Leah looks up at Danny.

Shut the fuck up, she says, what do you think you would've done? Danny looks over at the three boys standing around him.

I'll tell you what I would've done, he says. Leans down close to me. Sleeve still yanked up. His breath against my face. I would have killed those fucks, he says. Easy as that. He snaps his fingers. I keep my head down because now I'm shaking and the paste has worn off, my mouth weeping, I can feel my heart beating in my tongue, I keep my hands on my knees and Danny stands back up. Leah looks up at him, tells him to fuck off, and he sticks up his middle finger, shoves it toward her, calls her a bitch, calls me a pussy and then he and the other boys leave and go up to the party.

Leah leans over and clutches my forearm. It's shaking there holding my knees.

Don't listen to him, she says, he's a shit, you know that. She touches the back of my head. I nod. Bring a hand up to my lips and when I pull it down my fingers are red. I lean over and drag my hand across the grass. I spit. All blood. Leah looks over at me and doesn't say anything. She takes my hand and pulls me up. Walks me around to the passenger side of the car and opens the door.

ON A FRIDAY in mid-October Brett and I go to this place called DeBordieu. We have these friends, three sisters, whose dad's a rich tax lawyer who has a house that he lets us use sometimes. We're meeting about fifteen people there but I'm going because Leah is there and because all I do is think about her.

When we get to the house everyone's already drinking. Sitting around this long table on the second floor. Playing circle of death, a card game that makes you drink a lot. Brett and I both sit down at the table. Brett hands me a beer.

AFTER EIGHT BEERS I'm stupid. I can't see straight. I'm blabbering. I'm thinking about Leah the whole time.

And for the first time in a long while I don't hurt. The ulcers have healed. I can talk without drooling. I can eat without wincing. At the long table it's me and Brett, Justin, Mackie, Tom and Rick. Rick deals you a card and you have to say whether the next one will be high or low and if you lose you have to drink this gold rum. Brett loses the first time. Takes a shot and says go again. He loses again and after the shot he has to lean over and concentrate so he won't throw up. I lose the first time and the rum burns, I feel the blood rise in my face, hold my hands out to my sides like I'm trying to balance and I have to be very still so I won't puke.

Tom wins.

Justin loses. Runs to the bathroom.

Mackie loses. Wipes his mouth after the shot.

What? he says and he's all calm like he just drank water.

Rick calls us all pussies. Except for Mackie.

So fuck you, man, Brett says, your turn. Slams the deck.

All right, Rick says, bring it on, and Brett throws him a card.

Jack.

Low, Rick says, and the next card's high (queen) and then he's bringing the shot up to his mouth, gold in the light, he takes it, looks at us and pukes all over the table.

AT THREE TWENTY-EIGHT, me with Leah at the long table. I've watched her the whole time, moving around the room, putting hair behind her ears, changing the music when she doesn't like it, drinking something dark red. Rick passed out on the table. My brother gone. Mackie punched a hole in a bedroom door after he found out Justin was making out with this girl and now he's gone.

Leah and I are the only ones awake. We're listening to beach music which always gets played here, Otis Redding and the Spinners and the Platters, all these bands my parents love.

I tell Leah we should go on the beach. She's peeling the label off a beer. Looks over at me.

I'm not going to put the moves on you, I say. I promise. And she nods yes, we take the long steps leading down from the porch through sand dunes, grass tilting, the air thick with salt.

It's dark on the beach. We sit in the wet sand and for a long time we don't say anything. We smoke cigarettes and watch the flat water. And then Leah stands up, knocks the sand from her jeans. I stand up, too, and when I do I rise into her mouth, it's just there, her hands behind my head, my hands on the small of her back and the rain begins, it comes down soft and warm, slicks our faces, our hair, our arms, but we just stay there all locked up and then I pull back from her. I take her hand. She pulls me down. I touch her wet cheeks with both hands. Close my eyes. Hold my breath and wait for her mouth. She kisses me again and then pulls back, turns her head down and places it against my chest. She wraps her legs between mine and we stay like that, tangled and covered with sand and rain, until it's light.

LEAH'S VOICE LIKE a sigh. The phone trembling in my hands.

I tell her I love her and I mean it this time, I do, because I've said it before, said it because it sounded nice, said it because the words hovered thick between me and a girl named Sarah Hughes. I could see them. Hold them. But now I'm saying these words on a telephone and it's different. It's the only true thing I know.

But she doesn't say anything. She breathes into the phone. I tell her again.

What do you want me to say? she says.

I want you to say it back, I say, I want you to say it's true.

I can't, she says, it's not like that, how I feel and all.

The beach, I say, you know the rain and the sand, it was important, I mean like something that happens once.

A kiss, she says, that's what it was and I want to say no no it was so much more than our mouths and bodies, it was like God and I want to tell her she makes me feel safe, like I want to be inside her, like I want to be the last thing she hears before she falls asleep but my voice is shaking and all that comes out are these clumsy words.

Please, I say, please.

I can't, she says and then I'm sobbing, placing one hand against the cold windowpane in my parents' living room and through my handprint the oaks outside are still in the cold dark and Leah hangs up. I hold the phone to my ear, my face wet and streaked, I listen and wait for her voice to come back, her mouth, her words like light, but the phone hums silent.

WHEN I GO to sleep I have this dream:

Faceless men crouched low and moving on elbows and knees toward the windows, the doors of my parents' home. And I'm the only one there, crouched low in the corner of my bedroom, clutching my father's rusted twenty-two. Fingers claw at the windows and then I'm holding the gun toward the doorway, waiting for a body to fill it and it does, this black outline, and I'm pulling the trigger, it clicks, it clicks and nothing comes. I pull the trigger again, I pull it again, and in the dark of my room I hear only the sound of my breath, the drop of the hammer.

I wake up sweating with my legs pulled up against my chest. Shaking.

ON A THURSDAY in mid-November my left ear bursts.

I'm taking a bath holding my nose with my fingers trying to pop my ear like on the airplanes because it's been stopped up all week. I've been asking people to repeat themselves, tilting my head toward them, always standing on their left side so my good ear faces them. I can feel the heavy fluid in my head. I push the air through my nose into my head, I push until I can feel it leaking from my ear and then it all comes in a rush, this blood streaming from my ear into the water mixing red and yellow in my lap and it won't stop. I hold a hand to the ear and the blood runs through my fingers. Call my mother but the door is locked. She pounds on it, I stand up naked and dripping, a hand against my ear and the blood falls onto the tiles, leaves a trail. I unlock the door and go back to the bath, my mother comes in, sees the blood, me clutching my ear, she bends low beside the bath, pulls tissue in a handful, presses it against my ear and when it soaks through she gets more and does it again and she's a nurse and has always fixed me and she tells me that it will be all right like she always does but I know it won't.

THE DOCTOR SAYS I have a ruptured eardrum, and a broken bone in my inner ear. From head trauma, he says. He is old with thick glasses, he is called Dr. Deckle and usually in his office I'm bent over the table with my pants around my ankles, a nurse sticking a needle into my ass but now the nurse is holding gauze beneath my ear to catch the blood and the doctor's looking in my ear with the small flashlight. When he's done he steps back and tells me this is what happened:

Fluid gathered around the broken bone in my inner ear. The incus. Shaped like a club. It gathered there until it ruptured the eardrum. Split the thin tissue and poured out.

THIS IS WHAT I do:

Take antibiotics for the infection.

Leave cotton balls in my ear (changed every hour when soaked) for three weeks.

AFTER THE FLUID and the blood stop, my left ear is silent.

BRETT NEVER TELLS me that he's going to Clemson without me. Going ahead with this plan we made four months ago. I don't ask him either. I can't go now and he knows it. I didn't even fill out the application. We don't really talk about him leaving and me staying, we just see it coming, and I hate it even though I know it's what has to happen.

ON NEW YEAR'S EVE I am drunk. Stumbling from the beer. I look at Leah from across the bonfire. Raising a beer to her mouth, laughing, I want to fall in front of her, put my arms around her legs. Brett is behind her, his face also lit orange. He touches her shoulder. They both turn, flame against their backs, they laugh, leave the dark gathering around them and then I see him open the door to the house. She passes in front of him. The door falls shut.

I drop my beer into the fire and it hisses.

WHEN I SEE Brett and Leah again I know. They stand a few feet apart from each other. I know what they've been doing. And the alcohol inside me has made me dizzy and mad, I'm running the scene over in my mind—this girl I begged to love me, my brother in a back room, mouths locked, his hands behind her back, her hands against his face. And standing there beside the fire my brother's face is flushed red. I stare and I want him to see my eyes, I want him to know that I know what he's been doing but he doesn't look through the flame.

I WALK AROUND the edge of the fire toward Leah after Brett walks off because I can't stand still anymore. I put my hand around her forearm and look at her.

What the fuck? I say. She looks at me like I'm crazy. I let my hand drop. I'm still staring at her.

What, she says, what do you want?

Him, I say. Point to my brother. You and him?

Yeah, she says. Turns her eyes toward the fire. Yeah.

Why, I mean?

Okay. You have got to leave me alone. I'm sorry you're sad. I'm sorry about all that happened to you. But it's not you and me. It was just one kiss.

I know. But my brother.

So what? she says and my head is lolling, hands shaking, and all that comes out is mumbling, goddamn you I say goddamn you goddamn you.

She looks at me with hard eyes.

What?

I said goddamn you. She turns to leave.

No, fuck you. Fuck you. I scream it.

Fuck fuck fuck you. Fuck you. Motherfuck you. She doesn't turn and everyone gathered outside is staring me down. My brother comes over and I'm singing it now, fuck you, fuck you, over and over, this chant, this prayer. He takes my arm, I look at him, jerk my arm away, fuck you I say, point my finger at his face, fuck you, I throw my beer against a wall of the house. Brett grabs my arm again, tells me it's time to leave, pulls me while I'm still muttering it, fuck you, and he opens the passenger side door to his car, ducks my head and sits me down. He pulls onto the highway and inside the car it's dark and I'm not saying anything, I can feel his eyes on me.

Listen, he says, and I tell him to shut his fucking mouth. He sighs, drops his palms against the steering wheel. Listen, goddammit, he says and I turn to look at him. I point.

You knew, you fuck, I say, and you did it anyway. He shakes his head.

I start wailing inside the car slamming my hands against the glass. Brett pulls the car over to the side of the road. Turns the headlights off.

All you did was kiss, he says. I don't say anything. Fuck, man, he says, I didn't know you liked her so much. I wouldn't have done it, you know? I didn't know. I didn't.

Then I'm limp and heaving, he leans over and places a palm flat against my head, runs it backward and I can't stop crying.

Fuck, man, he says, and I know that I'm too much for him, that I'm too hard to be around.

For a long time we sit on the side of the cracked highway, me crying, him running his hand over my head and when cars pass their headlights burn white, the air they gather shakes the car.

TWO DAYS BEFORE he leaves Brett tells me he wants to know what's true. We're sitting in a bar, four in the afternoon, a table in the corner smoking cigarettes and drinking beer.

True about what? I say.

About anything. Your thing.

No one knows what to call my thing. Here are the names:

My mother: your abduction.

My father: the incident.

And then: The kidnapping. The robbery. The choking. The shit-kicking. The trunk thing. The woods thing. This thing. And I don't know what to call it, I just say what happened to me, that thing that happened.

Brett stubs a cigarette. Pulls another and lights it.

Did you see something?

Like what?

Like light. Or God. Your life.

No. Nothing like that.

Brett turns and looks over the bar, the dense smoke, the heads slouched over drinks, the dim light in the place. He blows a mouthful of smoke.

Saw a fox, I say.

A fox, he says.

Yeah. It talked.

Brett just looks at me. I mash the cigarette.

Asked me to stay there, I say.

I turn my head toward the bar and then back to Brett.

You want another beer? I say.

So? he says.

What?

The fox.

Yeah. It talked. Told me to stay there in the field. I didn't know how to get out and I was asking it but it kept telling me to stay there. Then it ran. But that was it, I mean, that's all I saw.

Brett finishes his beer. Stares down at the table. He hands me a cigarette, the ashes collected on the wood between us, white neon in the window.

MY PARENTS TELL him good-bye.

My father is smiling. My mother is trying not to cry. Got her arms crossed over her chest. We say this prayer together all standing in a circle holding hands, my mother's face clenched with the sobs saying please be with my boy protect him and my father calmly saying please be with my boy protect him and my youngest brother Matthew saying flatly dear God be with Brett and he's sixteen and in another place thinking of his friends and parties and this doesn't even make him blink and when it's my turn I just say please be with Brett, God, please take care of him but the whole time inside my head I'm saying please make him stay.

I keep opening my eyes and looking over at this picture of Brett and me while my mother and father say more prayers. We are small, maybe four and five, and we are straddling a cannon. A brick building behind us. Brett has on an orange shirt that says Clemson. He has on blue jeans. A baseball cap pulled down over his eyes. It says Clemson also. I have on the same thing. Brett's in front. I'm leaning my head to the side. And it's all there in the picture, and it's in my blood, this place my grandfather went, this place my father went, this place we are supposed to be together.

And then we all say amen. My mother and father hold Brett for a long time. He pats them on the shoulders, says I'm fine, I'll be fine. My mother keeps her arms crossed. My father nods.

AND AFTER THAT it's me and him in the driveway. On a Monday. Five days after New Year's.

Brett leans against his stuffed car. Arms crossed over his slim chest. All the clothes and sheets and a stereo and speakers and books inside the car. I want to tell him that he can't go, that I need him here with me but I don't because I know he needs to go, to be out of this crumbling town. And I know I'm part of the reason he needs to go.

I've got my hands in my pockets. Staring down at the concrete. Leaves and pine straw in the driveway. The sky hard and bright. I take my foot and kick at the leaves.

So, he says.

Yeah, I say. Still looking down.

You'll be fine. He touches my shoulder. I look up at him.

I know.

You will. I promise. And you can come when you're ready.

Yeah. I shake my head. August. He squeezes my shoulder.

When you're ready.

Okay. When I'm ready. But don't worry about me. I want you to be good up there. I know you will. You'll be a rock star. I throw my arms up above my head.

Yeah?

Oh, yeah. Fucking rock star.

Okay, he says. And then we don't know what to say. He just looks at me and I just look at him and five days ago I called him a fuck but now I don't care, I just don't care because he's leaving.

And in this silence my brother is speaking to me. He's telling me I will be good, I will be fine and I believe him, and for the first time in a long while I feel like I can breathe.

Brett takes the keys from his pockets. Twirls them on a finger.

Guess I should go, he says.

Yeah, I say. Sure.

So.

So.

Call me, he says.

I will.

He puts a hand behind my neck and pulls me into his chest.

I STAND IN the driveway and watch him go. He backs out. Moves up to the stop sign that borders the main road. Turns the blinker left. He doesn't look back.

I run to the sidewalk and watch his car. In the traffic, the rush of metal and tire, my brother's car grows small until I can't see it anymore.

4

RETT CALLS ON a Thursday. Four days after he left. Tells me he's going to join a fraternity. Kappa Sigma, he says and the whole time he's saying this to me I want to say why? (even though we went to fraternity parties because there was nothing else to do, we always made fun of them, fucking sheep we said, a bunch of fucking sheep) but I don't say anything because he sounds happy.

Nice people, he says. Really good guys.

Oh, yeah?

Yeah.

Well, okay.

Going to a bar tonight with them. Place called TD's.

Cool.

I think so. They're different than I thought, you know? They've been schmoozing me and this kid named Wes. And I'm meeting people. This place is fucking huge.

Yeah?

Really. Fucking huge. But this is making it easier.

Good. I told you.

What?

You'd be a rock star.

Whatever.

Told you.

Yeah. You did. But I'm not really a rock star.

Close, man. Real close. This is like the contract and all. The signing.

He laughs. Okay okay. The signing.

Fucking rock star.

Shut up.

Fucking rock star.

And then he says later and I say later and he hangs up the phone.

I GO TO Clemson to visit Brett on a weekend in March. Even though I wanted to go earlier, I didn't because I knew he needed the distance. He needed to figure things out. And part of me is scared that he'll be different, that the school will have changed him.

Clemson: air all wet from rain, dead leaves still scattered and piled against trees and buildings. Brett lives in a dorm called Johnstone, where my grandfather lived, and where my dad lived when he went here. The first thing I think when I see the building is that it should be condemned. It's tilted like it wants to keel over. Three stories with cracked windows and rusted air-conditioning units in each window. Torn stairwells on each side of the building enclosed by head-high fencing. I open a door on one corner of the building, the smell hits me in the face, the damp, the sweat. On the stairwell I pass boys in shorts and sleeveless shirts talking about weights, on the walls in black it says this among other things: fuck you Johnstone.

Brett's room is on the second floor and there are murals of cartoon characters painted along the hall, Bugs Bunny and Daffy Duck, Elmer Fudd, Road Runner, all these Looney Tunes with jungle backgrounds behind them. I knock on Brett's door and I hear the music inside, fast punk rock, a band called Screeching Weasel and he opens the door, throws his arms around my neck.

Man, he says, I'm glad to see you.

Me, too, I say. I mean good to see you. Not me.

Yeah. He holds the door open. I walk in. Inside the room there's a sink on one wall with a mirror, bunk beds on the other wall, a coffee table in the middle, two wooden wardrobes in the back corners. Neither of us has lived in a dorm before. At the last school we lived at home. Brett's got a poster from the movie *Reality Bites,* it's Ethan Hawke and Winona Ryder leaned in close. Brett sits down on the bottom bed. Hands on his knees.

This is where I live, he says.

Yeah it's cool, I say.

I sit down on the coffee table. The window is open. Someone yells from below, says Brett, Brett. Brett turns the music down, goes over to the window and leans out. He doesn't say anything. Someone yells get down here. Brett turns and looks at me.

Come on, he says.

Where? I say.

Gotta go down for a minute.

OUT ON THE sidewalk a guy sticks his hand out to Brett and Brett takes it.

Hey man, Brett says, this is my older brother and the guy holds out a hand toward me.

James Autrey, he says. I give my hand, he shakes it firm. Brett standing with his hands on his hips.

James's my big brother, he says. He means Kappa Sigma big brother, who, Brett's told me, is a person who looks out for you in the fraternity.

James looks at me and I want to tell him to fuck off but I don't.

Heard a lot about you, he says. I nod and then he's done with me, he turns to Brett, holds up a finger.

One second, he says, takes Brett over a few feet. He's got his arm around Brett's shoulders, mouth close to his ear, and Brett's nodding. They come back over to me.

Good to meet you, James says.

Likewise, I say. He turns to go and when he's down the sidewalk a bit Brett cocks his head toward the dorm entrance and we go and open the door.

On the stairwell Brett says that guy's pretty nice.

Yeah, I say, he seemed nice.

I gotta go do something, he says.

What?

Go pick up his girlfriend and take her over to his place.

Why?

Just because. He's my big brother.

I nod. I am jealous.

Inside Brett's room he pulls a white T-shirt over his head, puts on a navy short-sleeve collared shirt. Tucks it in.

Gotta dress up? I say.

Yeah, he says, we always have to look all right, you know?

Yeah, I say. Brett looks in the mirror. Runs hands back through his hair. Turns and looks at me.

I really don't want to do this, he says.

Sucks, I say.

Sure as fuck does. He holds one hand out. Can I borrow your car? he says. An hour tops. Don't feel like calling anybody right now for a car.

Yeah, man, I say, fumble in my pockets, pull out the keys and drop them into his hand.

You be all right here? he says.

Sure, I say.

After I'm done we'll hang out. Go to a movie or something.

Okay.

I tell you what, he says. That fucker doesn't know what he's got coming.

What fucker?

James. He's going to get his tomorrow. Kidnap.

I look at him. Squint my eyes.

It's this thing we do. The pledges. We ambush someone who gives us shit and put them in the back of a truck. Blindfold them. Make them drink a shitload until they get sick.

Oh.

I mean we're gonna fuck him up.

You guys can do that?

Sort of an unwritten rule. A tradition.

Sure. I look down at the floor.

Oh, fuck, man. He looks at me hard.

What?

I'm sorry.

What?

Kidnapping shit. I didn't even think about it.

It's okay. I'm over it.

Really?

Kind of.

You sure you'll be okay here?

Yeah. I'm sure.

Brett opens the door. Turns back to me. One hand still on the
door.

An hour, he says. I promise.

Yeah, man, I say. Wave him away. Go, I say. Brett nods his
head and closes the door.

THAT NIGHT WE go off campus to a movie theater because
Brett says no one will be able to find him there. Back in Brett's
room we turn off the ringer on the phone. I fall asleep to the
sound of someone's music playing down the hall and I leave in
the morning like I'd planned, before Brett wakes up, because I
know he has things to do, and in the car on the way home, when
I think about Clemson, it feels good, like where I should be.

THIS SEMESTER I'M making good grades, a three point zero.
I've forced the smile and the breath from my head.

It is this simple: I pretend it was a dream. Nobody talks
about it anymore. My father. My mother. Matthew. Everyone

is silent. And part of me knows that this will find me later, that it will hunt me down and run through me. But all the time I'm thinking about Clemson, about being normal and doing what Brett does. I let all of it stay quiet.

IN APRIL WE all go to DeBordieu again and Brett comes even though he's away at school. Brett brings this guy Chance McInnis, a kid we grew up with who's a brother in his fraternity.

When Brett and Chance get to the beach house it's like they're different kinds of people, like they're somewhere doing something important and even though I know what they're doing isn't important, I can't help but feel that they're stars or something. Everybody stares at them when they come in, already drunk because they pounded beers in the car the whole way down. Like they know something about the world that we don't.

After a while, Brett goes and sits in a trash can. Legs out over the edge, his head resting against the back. Drinking his beer. I'm staring at this girl who I know would break me if I loved her but I can't help it. I look over at Brett. Holds his hand out to me. I can tell something's off about him, his eyes wild and swimming with the alcohol. I go over and take his hand. He looks up at me and tells me he loves me, tells me he's sorry. I know he's telling me he's sorry for not being there that night. I shake my head and say it's cool. He keeps holding my hand.

No, he says. It's not.

Yeah, it is, I say. He rubs his eyes, his temples. I'm sorry for being fucked up, I say. He shakes his head.

You aren't fucked up. I'm fucked up. He smiles. Not like

mentally or anything, he says. I'm just drunk. I pull him up out of the trash can and he wobbles. I put my hands on his shoulders and he shrugs them away.

I'm fine, he says. Light-headed that's all. He takes a pull from the beer. Points over at Chance, who's sitting on the couch with this girl.

Now he, Brett says, is a sonofabitch. He looks nice and all but he's a fucking sonofabitch. Break me in half if I told him that though. Big fat bitch.

Brett's words sliding from his mouth like spit.

He looks at me. Smiles.

I'm sorry, he says. I nod.

Chance tells Brett to get his ass over. Brett stumbles over, sits down next to Chance. I look at the girl I've been watching the whole time. Leaned against a wall across the room. Pulling hair behind her ears. Cocking a hip to one side. I go into the kitchen and find some vodka. I hate vodka but there's nothing else but beer and I need something to make me brave. The shot glass coming to my lips. Again. Once more for luck. I chase it with the beer.

SHE'S STANDING BY the stereo, looking for a compact disc. I wipe my mouth and go over and when I'm there I touch the small of her back and she turns her face up. Smiles. Eyes wobbling.

What do you like? she says.

Anything, I say. She holds up a disc. Sam Cooke again. I nod. I feel her hand graze mine. It's light and we test each other that way with our fingers against each other and then I put my fingers through hers and she pulls me toward the porch.

OUTSIDE WE DANCE, and the alcohol has made me bold and when I kiss the girl it's like every bad thing that came before doesn't matter. I keep my eyes open the whole time.

THE MUSIC'S DONE. I take the girl to a bed, lay her down and pull the sheets up over her. She leans up and kisses me hard, drops her head back down and I stand there and I wish she'd love me but I know it would be like before with Leah. This random moment. I'd make her sick, she'd hate me, I'd cry for days. So I watch her fall asleep and she's perfect.

I GO INTO the bathroom and Brett's laid down sideways on the vanity, arms in one sink, feet in the other, torso across the flat middle. The long mirror at his back. I stare at him for a long time there in the sinks, watching him breathe and his breath is slow. His face flushed red. Stubble around his cheeks and mouth. And he's got this small stream of blood running from his right nostril. It's slow and dried on his upper lip. I take tissue and wipe his nose, his upper lip. Wait for the blood to come back. And when it doesn't I bend down, put one arm under his legs and the other beneath his shoulders. Pick him up. He puts his arms around my neck, rubs his head into my chest. Leaves a red stain on my shirt. I take him into a bedroom, lay him down. Pull off his shoes. Put the pillow beneath his head. A trash can beside his face. I sit down against the wall and watch him. He stirs, cracks one eye and looks over at me.

Love you, man, he says.

Yeah, I love you, I say and then he's sleeping again. Lamplight in one corner of the bedroom. The tissue still in my hands, I take a thumb and run it over the dried blood. Against the wall I watch my brother and I know now even more that I want to be with him at Clemson, be like we were in the picture. I decide then that I'm going to go to Clemson and I'll pledge his fraternity. Even though something inside thinks it's wrong, I make it quiet. I hold the tissue and watch my brother breathe until my eyes close.

I GET ACCEPTED to Clemson in early May. Brett comes home. Moves to the beach. I stay at my parents'. To earn money, I say. But really I don't want to leave yet. I tell myself that I need the time because it's all I've got left.

I take a job delivering flowers. To hospitals. Funeral homes. And all summer it's me and death and sickness, opening the doors of hospital rooms, an old man or woman alone with the tubes and the machines clicking beside them and the smell like urine and disinfectant, I take the flowers, the vases, the cards, I place them on the tables beside the beds and leave.

At the funeral homes I pull up to the back, open the door for deliveries and it's always caskets and flowers and pink carpet and old wood.

IN EARLY AUGUST, Brett and I leave for Clemson. On the interstate, fields fade to red clay and broken rock. Small towns named Pender, Union, and Newberry along the way. Every so often we pass crosses made from wood or PVC pipe and they're topped with weathered plastic flowers. Skid marks nearby. A crumpled shoulder guard. The crosses are barely visible, placed at the edge of woods next to a scarred tree. Sometimes a name on a wooden sign attached to the cross. Sometimes none.

I am trailing my brother closely and my car rattles when it hits sixty-five. Brett doesn't look in his rearview every so often like I wish he would to make sure I'm still here.

I KEEP THINKING about what Brett knows, how he's leading me somewhere I need to be, and I feel like I'm doing the right thing. For a while I play the Clash really loud and it makes me feel good.

After I play four CD's I turn on the radio. A NASCAR race is on and I don't even like car races but it's nice to listen to the voice and the occasional hum of cars. But the cars make me think about the crosses on the side of the road and how small they are and I can't stop and I shake when I think about the place I'm going. Even though I think it's a good move, I know I'm carrying this thing with me that will fuck me sooner or later. I clench my mouth and hold my breath, concentrate on the road. Clemson is seventy miles away but I can already see it waiting for me.

The Star and Crescent shall not be worn by every man, but only by him who is worthy to wear it.

Kappa Sigma Credo,
Bononia Docet, Kappa Sigma Pledge Manual

Ernest Howard Crosby, a brother and poet, wrote:
> No one could tell me where my soul might be;
> I searched for God but He eluded me;
> I sought my brother out and found all three.

Bononia Docet, Kappa Sigma Pledge Manual

5

AFTER BRETT AND I leave the interstate and take the Clemson exit, the tiger paws start. On the asphalt, footprints painted orange, five feet long, five feet wide, like monster tigers have walked there. I could lie down on them with only my head sticking over the edge of the toes.

We pass fields, cows bending to the grass. Some sit, and I remember what my father told me about sitting cows, that it means rain. But the sky is clear and bright.

We stop at a gas station called Tiger Mart. A square building painted orange, Go Tigers in black lettering above the door-frame.

Inside the store, Brett and I buy cigarettes. I stuff the receipt in my pocket because I've started to keep things. Mostly just receipts and change, but anything really. A glass bluebird from my parents' house. A tiger cut out from an Exxon gas card. Things like that.

Outside we lean against Brett's car and smoke.

Too hot to smoke, he says. He looks up.

Yeah, I say. Brett wipes his forehead with the back of his palm. Pulls the smoke. Drops it on the ground and crushes it with a foot. Looks over at me.

You ready? he says. He knows I'm nervous. And even though things feel okay between us now, they're still different. I know he feels like he needs to look after me, but part of him is broken too. The thing that happened to me a year ago is his thing too. And he is aloof most of the time. Stays in his head. Speaks only when necessary. And even though he doesn't say anything I can feel his apprehension about me coming here, his nervousness, the way he smokes hard, the way he turns his head down the road toward Clemson in the afternoon heat.

Sure, I say. I'm ready. Look down the road and squint my eyes. Brett pulls out another cigarette and lights it and I do too because that's what we do when we're nervous. Brett opens his door and gets in his car. Through the glass, the cigarette on his lips, smoke filling the inside of the car.

THE MONSTER TIGER paws are painted the whole way into town. We cross under a brick railroad arch, the trees on both sides green with summer. Brett tells me the weather in Clemson works like this: in the summer and into fall it is bone-hot, heat rising opaque from the asphalt, grass burnt, soil fired hard. And when fall is over, around late October, the heat stops and the hard cold begins.

When we get to Main Street, I know I'm there. Shops on both sides. Everything related to the school—Tiger Pharmacy,

Tiger Sports Shop, Tiger Sports Bar. Orange everywhere—burnt-orange brick, signs, doors, walls painted orange.

When Main Street ends there's an open field. Girls in bathing suits laid out in the grass. Shirtless boys throwing footballs and Frisbees.

Behind the field, the campus. Everything the same dull burnt-orange brick as the buildings downtown. A clock tower standing over everything. A right turn at the end of Main and a left past a soccer field, the football stadium called Death Valley. Lights at the top of the stadium like fists.

The stadium is called Death Valley for the obvious reason, it's meant to be a fearsome place where teams come to play and leave bleeding, but also because a legendary Clemson football coach, Frank Howard, got a rock from Death Valley, California, and had it attached to a waist-high monument at the place where the football players enter the stadium. Told the players that they couldn't touch his rock unless they came to send people home limping. Players rub Howard's Rock for good luck and to remind themselves that they are there to inflict pain.

Cars everywhere, dropping off, pulling in, turning left, backing up, all at once. We pull into a parking lot. Find two spaces beside each other even though the place is packed. Everyone pulling things from trunks, picking them up, walking hunched toward dorms.

We get out and Brett points to a brick building.

That's the back of our dorm, he says.

It's three stories. Brett tells me these things: our dorm is part of six buildings, three on each side of a courtyard. We're going to live on opposite sides of the same dorm. The first two floors and some of the third are all fraternity kids. Phi Delts on one side, Kappa Sigmas on the other. The third floor is a mix of fraternity kids and whatever other guys get dropped there. Fraternity dorms are all guys and sorority dorms are all girls. He's on the first floor on the Kappa Sigma side, I'm on the third floor on the Phi Delt side.

I nod. Kids moving up the stairs carrying clothes, televisions, stereos, mini-refrigerators.

We'll get our shit later, Brett says. Too many fucking people right now.

I can't stop smoking. Neither can Brett. He starts walking toward the dorm, Daniel Hall, and I follow him.

IT'S MONDAY, THE day before classes start, and I'm in my dorm room. My room has tall wardrobes on both sides of the door. A window on the far wall. My bed on the left side. My roommate's on the right. If I stand between our beds I could touch both if my arms were cut off at the elbow. My roommate has this loft thing that he made. It's like a bunk bed without the bed underneath. Instead there's a small futon and our twelve-inch television, a mini-refrigerator and a stereo. On each side of the window is a desk. Bookshelves on both walls, but no posters. My roommate's this kid Greg I know from home, not someone I know really well, just someone who needed a roommate like I did.

I had to have a major so I chose Studio Art. Photography, painting, drawing, all that. I'm a junior. Brett's a sophomore and he hasn't decided what his major is.

But there, sitting in my room, I start thinking about being an art major, and how much all the supplies cost and how I don't have that much money and I don't know where an art supply store is so I decide art's not for me. I also figure art's not for me because I'm sticking with my idea about pledging Brett's fraternity and I know it'll take up a lot of time and all the art classes are three hours long two times a week and I've got two of those plus two other classes. Brett and I talked about me pledging Kappa Sig and he says he wants me to if it's what I really want. I tell him yeah it's what I want. Fraternity rush starts on a Sunday, in less than a week.

I GO TO the bookstore after I decide not to be an art major and decide to be an English major because the books you get to read look cool.

I have a friend from back home who lives one floor down from me in Daniel and he's in Phi Delt and after I leave the bookstore I go back to his room and on his computer I drop all my art classes and sign up for English classes, one American Lit and one British Lit, and that's all I have to do to change my major. I have to take three other classes. Geology, Statistics, Religion.

I go back to the bookstore and buy the books and put the receipt in my right pocket.

CLASSES GO WELL the first week and I like the English classes and the Religion class but not the other ones so much. I go home on Friday because I know it's my last chance before all the fraternity shit. I've got to leave early Sunday morning because the first rush events start Sunday afternoon.

At home I sleep like the dead. I wake on Saturday and I have to get some new glasses because mine are bent from sleeping with them on. I get these small black-rimmed glasses. Keep the receipt.

After I get the glasses I'm at a stoplight. And then there's a face against my window, a fist tapping the glass, and I know I shouldn't roll down the window but I do it anyway, this guy says a ride, can I get a ride and the light turns green, all these horns blowing behind me, I say yeah get in, lean over and unlock the passenger side door. And I know I shouldn't. I know it but there's this part of me that wants to. This part of me that wants to be scared. Like I can fix everything if I do it. And he's sitting there beside me. I don't look over. I start to drive.

The man asks if I can take him up the street.

Sure, I say. Not far though. I have to be somewhere.

Okay, he says and then I look over at him. His hair is black, greased, hands folded in his lap like he's praying. Got dirt all in the nails.

He tells me he's a preacher and I say oh, yeah, I know about preachers, my dad's a preacher and he says what church and I say Highland Park Methodist and he nods his head, oh, yeah, that's a fine church, yeah, a fine church.

So have you been washed? he says.

Washed? I say.

Cleansed. Blood of the lamb.

Sure. I've been washed. We've gone a few miles, my hands shake and I know I shouldn't have done this, it hasn't fixed anything, and I don't want to be scared anymore. I stop the car. Right there in the middle of the road. Cars blaring their horns at me. I keep my eyes straight. Hands on the wheel.

Get out, I say. I don't look at him.

You'll die, you know, he says. God just told me. You'll die.

Okay. Yeah. I'll die. Get out. I don't look at him.

Fire. You'll burn.

Get out. I look over at him. Get out, I say. He starts to open the door.

God punishes those who ignore his servants, he says. I'm his servant.

Get out.

You'll burn. In a wreck. On the way home. I promise. You'll end in fire. He gets out of the car. Keeps a hand on the door.

Fuck you, I say. Dirty fuck.

He leans back in, points a finger at me and I press the gas with him there holding on to the door. He falls. Crumples on the sidewalk.

On the way home I'm shaking and thinking about what I just did and how I was right to be scared, how it didn't help, how people are fucked everywhere, how I got lucky and how maybe it's just a matter of time before my luck runs out.

AFTER I TOLD Brett I definitely wanted to pledge Kappa Sig he seemed apprehensive, but he also seemed happy and thought it would be a good idea for me to be around some of his fraternity brothers before rush started.

At a lake off campus the week before rush, we went to a rope swing and took turns showing how unafraid we were to swing to its highest point, forty feet above the lake, let go, flail our arms the entire way down, crash with a sharp split into the brown water. There was a tree stump buried directly below the point where we would naturally fall. Someone had tied an orange life jacket to its branches so we'd know where it was. So we had to swing and pitch ourselves out past this stump to avoid breaking our legs. This one brother went over the stump headfirst. Landed with a thud. Seven times. Rose each time smiling, hair pasted to his scalp, skin slapped red and shining.

Sunday afternoon I'm at the first party of official rush after driving back from home early that morning. Brett standing a few feet away. Light from a small doorway falls in bright columns across his face and slight chest. His arms crossed, he is glowing and talking to a brother I recognize from the lake.

Everyone wearing name tags. And later, if I get a bid, remembering brothers' names becomes the most important thing. Not just first names. Last names. Majors. Hometowns. Everything.

AT CLEMSON THERE are no on-campus fraternity houses, only dorms. The fraternity dorms are all grouped together in a quad. The sororities are together too but they don't have a quad, just a bunch of buildings all beside each other, and this get-to-know-you thing on the Kappa Sigma hall just means we hang out on the side of our dorm where Kappa Sigmas live.

The Kappa Sigs serve finger food of the worst kind, pimiento cheese, ham, and barbecue sandwiches, plain potato chips, corn chips, tortilla chips and salsa, all piled into plastic bowls that look as if everyone here has groped them. There's plastic silverware. Not white plastic but a more elegant, clear version. Bottles of liquor on the table. A few two-liter soft drinks. The table covered with a red-and-white-checked tablecloth. Two coolers of ice at the foot of the table. One laid open with a plastic cup for dealing out ice, the other shut, says Kappa Sigma Mountain Weekend on top in red and green letters.

Will Fitch stands with a boy named Chris Sample, clutches a plastic cup in one hand, fumbles nervously in a pocket with the other. Wiry tufts of blond hair stick out from the side of his khaki hat. He doesn't look cool at all. Neither does Chris. He has his arms crossed over his chest, hands tucked beneath his armpits, he's trying to poke his chest forward. Make himself seem bigger. No dice, I say.

Will and Chris look like they shouldn't be here. Like they're lost. I wonder if I look like they do. They don't talk to anyone other than themselves. I dig out some ice with a cup. Trying to fix my own drink. I take Jim Beam and Coke, dabble a small amount of bourbon into the cup, quickly fill it with Coke so no one will see how little liquor I've poured.

MY BROTHER COCKS his head to one side, listens doggedly as a brother stresses a point with his hands. Brett looks over and waves me toward him.

I shake hands with the brother. He tells me his name is Ben Moore. He has three inches and forty pounds on me. He takes a sip of his drink and smiles. He swirls the liquid around. Rattles ice against plastic.

Pretty fun, huh? he says. I nod.

I can't think of anything to say. Turn awkwardly to my brother.

So? I say, look at Brett, hope that he'll get the conversation going. Ben walks away and begins to talk to someone else. Brett pulls me in close to the wall. I can smell the bourbon on his breath. Sharp and hot. I pull back a bit. He clasps my arm firmly at the bicep.

You have to meet these people, he says. Stares at me. I look away.

I'm serious, he says. Squeezes my arm. They aren't going to let you in just because you're my brother, you know? I mean it. These guys are funny about that stuff. Now go and shake some hands and make them want you, he says.

I nod, bring the Jim Beam and Coke to my lips and take a small swallow. The bourbon burns my throat. I crunch an ice cube in the back of my mouth and look around for someone to talk to.

RUSH WEEK LASTS from Sunday until Friday, when bids go out. Sunday I leave the Kappa Sigma thing and walk around the quad to some of the other fraternities, but they all seem the same, so I decide I might as well stick with Brett.

On Monday when there's nothing official to go to at Kappa Sigma, I go with Chance McInnis to a bar called TD's. Brett and I grew up with Chance and he wants me to be in the fraternity. Even though TD's isn't technically rush, it's important, because Chance is a brother, a popular one, and this whole rush thing is about being around brothers as much as possible.

Chance pounds on my door at nine-thirty. When I open it he's standing there all smiles and I hold out my hand. He takes it and places his other hand over our locked grip. When he lets go I tell him to go over and sit down.

Got to put on my shoes, I say. He sits on my bed and I sit in the metal desk chair at the back of my room. He looks around like he's trying to think of something to say to me. I begin to pull on one boot.

So this is a cool place, I say.

Oh yeah, he says. Plenty of pussy here. Says this like it hurts. I bend to tie both boots.

Yep, he says. Plenty plenty.

And that's a bad thing? I say and I know that he's leading me to ask what's wrong with him.

Nah, he says. I guess not. It's real good. He rubs a hand across his chin. Not for me though.

Oh yeah?

Yeah. Got this new girlfriend. Jill. Jill LaSalle. She's a Kappa.

That's good, I say but I don't really know if it's good or not. And it's going well?

Pretty good, he says. I mean I was doing pretty good. Kinda messed up today.

Yeah?

Yeah. She won't find out, I don't think, but I guess I feel bad. I didn't mean to, I mean I just went over to this girl's room to study. Marketing. We already got a test. Already. So I was just going to study. And I go over there and she opens the door in a bathrobe. A fucking bathrobe. I was like fuck but I couldn't just leave, you know, I had to study because of the test, right. I was like okay, Chance, this doesn't mean anything but the robe it was all silk, you know, I could see her tits through it. I sit down on the bed and she says she's sorry that she just got out of the shower and I'm like no it's cool and I start pulling my stuff out of my book bag all my notes and shit and I open my book and pretend to start looking at the chapters because she's not saying anything. I look up and she's just standing there in front of me. She lets the robe fall open right in front of my face, these big fucking tits right there. I didn't know what to do.

And? I say. What did you do?

I fucked her, he says. I feel bad, man. But I just couldn't help it. I mean the robe and all that. The tits.

Yeah, I say. The tits.

I look at Chance sitting there on my bed and he looks concerned. We get up to leave and we walk down the stairwell toward Chance's four-door Jeep that's parked behind the dorm. On the second flight down I look over at him.

So what was her name? I say.

Who? he says.

The girl.

Oh. Yeah. He rubs one hand along the chipped black railing. I don't remember, he says.

INSIDE TD'S THE smoke is thick and collects beneath the fluorescent lights. A few people at scattered round tables.

We sit at a long polished bar and Chance looks over at the bartender. He's wiping the inside of a glass with a towel. Chance snaps his fingers. The bartender looks up, comes our way and keeps wiping the glass.

What can I get you, bud? he says.

You know what I want, son, Chance says. Same over here. He nods at me. I hold up two fingers and mouth the word two. The bartender opens a gleaming metal cooler and pulls out two Budweisers. Twists the caps into a trash can beside the cooler, places the beers under two napkins in front of us. Chance hands him a ten.

Why do they always give you the napkins? Chance says. I shrug. Put the napkin in my right pocket. He looks at the bartender punching keys on a cash register.

Hey, he says. He snaps his fingers and the bartender looks up while he counts change.

Why do you always give us napkins? The bartender shrugs. He finishes counting the bills and walks back over to us. Throws the money down in front of Chance.

I don't know, the bartender says. Protect the wood. He knocks a fist against the bar.

Well, yeah, Chance says. This looks like strong wood though. Plus you wipe it all the time, right? The bartender wipes a spot beside Chance.

Yeah, he says. Drapes the towel over his forearm. I guess we do. Just the rules, man.

That's what they teach you in bartender school, huh?

Exactly. The bartender looks down at a page pinned under a clipboard and walks to the other end of the bar. Chance looks over at me and smiles.

I don't believe I like his attitude, he says. I laugh and take a pull from the beer.

AFTER AN HOUR the bar starts to fill and someone has played AC/DC on the jukebox. I'm on my fourth beer and Chance is on his seventh. He gets louder every time his mouth opens.

Damn, son, he says. Leans over. Breath hot and sweet from the beer. How many of those are you gonna smoke? He points at my cigarette. I blow smoke in his face, he fans it away and coughs.

Give me one, he says. I shake one from the pack and he takes it between his teeth, drops his lips around the filter. I bring the lighter up.

Thanks, he says. Blows a mouthful of smoke into my face. I don't flinch and he looks disappointed. He props his elbows against the bar railing. Two girls beside him. He looks over at them and then back at me. Points across his chest toward them. I tap my cigarette into the ashtray and shake my head. He looks puzzled.

I'm no good, I say.

What? he says over the music.

No good, I say again but he just shakes his head. He turns, starts talking to the girl beside him. He leans back and points at me. My hands start to shake and I rub them together. I crush my cigarette in the ashtray and push the stool out. I'm about to get down but Chance puts his hand flat against my chest.

Hold on, he says. Got somebody wants to meet you. I look over and the girls have gotten down from their stools and are standing in front of Chance and me. One girl's tall, the other a little shorter and they're both done up and have on tight clothes, small black pocketbooks draped over their shoulders. One girl looks at me and sticks out her hand. Her black hair reaches her shoulders.

Hi, she says. I give her my hand.

Hi, I say. Brad.

Michelle, she says. Chance leans in.

This is Jill, he says. I look at him. He skirts his eyes, coughs and shakes his head quickly because he doesn't want me to ask if this Jill is his girlfriend.

Hey, I say shaking her hand. Nice to meet you both.

Brad here's gonna be a Kappa Sig, Chance says. He places one hand on my shoulder. The girls nod and smile.

I hope, I say.

You hope? Chance says. You're a damn lock, boy. He slaps my back and turns toward the bar, holds up four fingers toward the bartender. Michelle climbs up onto the stool beside me. Places the pocketbook in front of her and the bartender brings over two beers. She looks into the pocketbook, pulls out a cigarette. I scoop my lighter up, bring the flame to the tip of her cigarette. She cups her hands around my hands, her eyes move up to my face and the flame makes her skin glow. I look away.

Thanks, she says.

Forget it, I say. Chance leaning into Jill with one hand on her small arm. She's smoking and nodding. Chance bringing the beer up to his lips. I look back over at Michelle.

So, I say. What year are you?

Freshman, she says. Lets out a mouthful of smoke. Fans the smoke away. You?

Junior, I say. I just transferred. She nods.

So you're gonna be a Kappa Sig, she says.

Well, I say. I hope. If things go well. I peel the edge of the label on my beer.

Oh, I'm sure you won't have a problem.

We'll see. Are you rushing?

Yeah. We're almost done. I think it's either Tri Delt or Kappa right now. I nod.

They're both really great, she says. I love the girls in both of them. I don't know how I'm going to decide.

They both sound good, I say.

Yeah, she says. It's just such an important decision. I look at her again with her small nose and black eyes. She smiles when she sees me looking at her and I turn away. She touches my arm.

It's okay, she says. You can look at me. I turn back toward her.

She brushes the hair back from my eyes.

You have a great face, she says. I look down at the beer and then back at her.

You too, I say. You have a great face too. She tucks one side of her hair behind an ear and twists the cigarette into the ashtray, reaches into her pocketbook and pulls out another.

Chain-smoker, she says. Puts the cigarette between her lips. Sorry.

No, I say. I am too, sometimes. I light her cigarette again. She exhales.

You want one? she says. I have my own but I nod and reach over to the pack she's holding. I light the cigarette and take a pull.

Thanks, I say. Turn my head up to blow the smoke at the ceiling. It hangs there tangled in the lights. I look over at Chance and he's kissing Jill, one hand resting on her waist. I look back over at Michelle. She runs a hand along my thigh and stares at me. I hunch over the bar because I'm getting hard. She holds the cigarette at shoulder level and I don't know what to say or do and this is the first time a girl in a bar has ever even touched me and we've barely talked and I don't even know her last name. I breathe in deep, take another pull from the cigarette and then the beer. I drink it fast, let it burn my tongue and throat. In the mirror behind the bar I can see my face, my nervousness, everything I know that's wrong about me. Michelle rubs my thigh and leans over toward my ear. Her wet lips graze my earlobe and I can feel her breath and the hand moving up and down my thigh and I turn my head back toward her and she's perfect there with her pursed lips and her chest rising and the smoke gathering around her through the lights and I know she can fix me, I can feel my fingers through hers, I know I'll wake up with her, I can see us maybe married and then I feel a hand on my back. Grabs my shirt and pulls me down from the stool.

Time to go, bud, Chance says and we're walking out of the bar and I'm trying to hide the fact that I'm hard walking hunched over and Chance pushes the door open. I look back and Michelle is smiling after me, crushing her cigarette. She uncrosses her legs and crosses them again the other way. Holds up one finger toward the bartender. Chance lets his hand fall away from my neck. We walk toward his car and I pat my pockets.

I forgot my cigarettes, I say. Chance reaches into his pockets.

Here, he says. Hands me a pack. Take these. I stole them from that whore.

What whore? I say. The girl you were making out with?

Chance turns and glares at me. Points his finger toward my chest. That, he says, was not meant to happen. I nod because I don't want to push him and because I need his vote, but also because I know that Michelle wouldn't have touched me if Chance hadn't told her I was going to pledge.

Don't say a word, he says.

I won't, I say. Swing my head back and forth. I swear. I don't want to leave but I just keep walking with my hands in my pockets and my head turned down to cracks in the sidewalk.

I can't be around all that shit, man, he says. It's too much. We stop beside his car and he pulls his keys from his pocket. I go around to the other side, wait for the lock to click. I open the door and get inside.

Inside the car Chance doesn't speak. He looks straight ahead. When we pull into the dorm parking lot he turns to me.

Listen, bud, he says. I'm sorry I snapped at you back there. And I'm sorry we had to leave. You didn't want that girl anyway. I've seen her around. She's a groupie.

I don't know what he means.

I kind of liked her, I say.

Yeah, he says, you would. You're new. But those girls just want a fraternity man. Especially a Kappa Sig.

It's like he's teaching me an important lesson.

Well, shit, he says, laying his hands across the steering wheel. Sometimes it's okay. Most of the time actually. You'll get more chances, I promise. You pledge and you'll get it all the time.

I place my hand on the car door and open it. Chance grabs my arm when I turn to go.

Don't say anything, okay? he says. The girlfriend. You know?

That's the last thing you need to worry about, I say. It's between you and me. Got stone lips. Fucking granite, man.

Chance smiles.

That's my boy, he says. He slides the gearshift into reverse.

Listen, he says. I'll make it up to you. I promise. Next time we go out it's all the groupie whores you can handle. I nod and shut the door and wave as Chance backs the car from the parking lot. He thumps over a raised parking guard and stops, looks around and starts back again. I stumble up the steps to my room.

I GET A BID.

I'm in Brett's room on the Kappa Sigma hall on Friday, the day after the vote to decide who gets in. Rush is quick. Pledge season is not. Brett shuts the door. I'm nervous because he looks serious. This is what he tells me: Last night the brothers went into the lounge to vote on me and came out after a few minutes. Brett was not allowed in because I'm his brother and he waited in the hall outside. A few brothers shook their heads as they piled out toward their rooms like something was very bad. Brett almost shit his pants. Ben Moore started to laugh when Brett grabbed him and Dixon Lynch slapped his back. Dixon said they were just fucking with him. Brett says he was actually scared for a minute. Brett says fuck the details. You're in. It's all that matters.

AFTER I LEAVE his room, I go and get the official bid in paper form from the Residency Life Office. They have someone there just to hand out bids. In my dorm room I stick the bid under my bed.

THE BROTHERS GIVE us a party. For being pledges.

On Saturday I sit on the concrete steps outside Daniel Hall and wait for Dave Reed. I know Dave from the town I lived in before Florence, a town called Summerville, and we start hanging out because it's good to know someone in the pledge class. Across the quad the KA hall is lit up, bodies moving in front of open windows. A Confederate flag is draped over someone's windowsill and someone's playing Lynyrd Skynyrd, bellowing the music out into the retreating daylight. Ben Moore says that KA's are rich-boy fucks. Pretty-boy faggots.

DAVE COMES AROUND the corner and slips under the branches of a small oak, brushes his hair back away from his face. The air heavy with leftover heat. Dave's dressed in khakis and a blue button-up. He stands there fumbling through his pockets.

So, he says. You ready? I look around and stay seated.

Yeah, I say. Sure.

Are you going to get up? I look at him. The sun dropping behind the dorm at my back, making a long shadow stretch behind Dave into the quad. It bends to his left and he shuffles his feet against the concrete, scrapes one heel and then the other like he's trying to tap-dance.

Nervous? I say.

He turns his head up from the ground. No, he says. No. He's lying. You?

Kinda. I rub my hands together. Yeah, I'm actually really nervous.

Maybe I am. A little. He scrapes another heel and then he bends to pick up a rock. He throws it toward a metal trash can to my right and it clangs off into the bushes. I pick up a rock at my feet and try the same throw. The bushes shake when it cuts straight through the leaves. Dave looks at me and smiles.

Can't throw, huh? he says.

Nah, I say. Never could.

I just got lucky. I can't throw either. He picks up another rock and throws it against the trash can.

Lucky, huh? I say. Still seated.

He shrugs. What do you think's gonna happen tonight? he says.

I suppose we'll get drunk.

Well, yeah. Besides that.

What do you mean?

I don't know. It's just that Chance used to come home and tell me stuff. Not much. Just stuff that wasn't good.

I think about Brett and how he's never really said anything other than I had to make people like me. And even though I've heard things from other people who rushed, I haven't taken it seriously. I've always seen it as goofy, like the movies or something—paddles, John Belushi, having to drink beer or take bong hits.

Yeah. I don't know. Maybe I got it wrong.

Probably, I say. You like all these guys?

Sure. I guess. They seem okay.

Okay or do you like them?

I like them. I guess I just don't know them that good yet to say whether I really like them. Why, do you? he says.

Sure, I say and turn back toward the ground.

I'm lying but I keep telling myself that I need these guys and that I will like them eventually. I need them to be normal. I need them to be like Brett.

They sure as shit have been nice, he says.

They have.

So, what's the big deal?

No big deal. I was just wondering. How you felt and all.

I'm cool if you're cool.

I'm cool.

Yeah?

Yeah.

Me too. I'm cool too.

We leave the quad and start down Main Street. Cars blowing by in the early darkness. We walk up the hills on Main Street and the sweat starts everywhere. I can feel it on my forehead and back. Beneath my arms. My chest tightens and I pull out a cigarette.

Man, Dave says looking over at me. You must have strong lungs.

No, I say. I don't. I just figure I might as well enjoy myself.

Right, he says. We stop and sit on a bench beside a Methodist church. It's all dark fat stones, the tall stained-glass window out front lit up, each piece shines with the light behind it. It's Jesus and he's standing there with his solemn face and his arms laid at his sides, the hands upturned and pushed out like he's offering something up. But there's nothing in his hands. I look at my own hands and they're empty and small, the kind of hands that girls hold theirs up to and curl the tops of their fingers over. I flick the cigarette onto the church grass and Dave gets up and runs over to it. He picks it up, mashes it on the bottom of his shoe and walks back over to me. He's still holding the butt.

What in the hell are you doing? he says. You shouldn't flick cigarettes in a churchyard.

Nobody saw it.

Yeah, but it's a sin or something. He moves past me and throws the cigarette into the road. Sits back down beside me and rests his forearms against his thighs, leans over and gathers his hands between them.

You should know better, man, he says.

I'm sorry, I say. Look over at him slouched beside me. Really. I'm sorry.

Okay, he says turning up to me. Just don't do it again.

Sure, I say. I promise.

He crosses his legs and leans back, stretches one arm behind the bench. Reaches forward and brushes his polished brown loafers. We get up and take the sidewalk again and it's just a ways to the apartment we're going to and underneath the oak and burning street lamps I light another cigarette.

WE GO TO an apartment complex where three sets of brothers live in three different apartments. We round the entrance and start down a steep hill. Hands in our pockets. In the parking lot people swarm around cars, hover beneath doorstep lights. Dave and I see the first brother slouched against a rusted brown Chevette and he's just standing there, a beer in one hand and a cigarette in the other. He turns his head when he sees us walking up.

Hello, boys, he says.

We nod. He turns the beer up and sucks the last bit. I wonder why he's leaning against this beat-up car by himself, sweating and staring at everyone. He wipes his forehead with the back of his palm.

Hot, he says. Hot as a whore in church. Dave laughs.

Go on and get a beer, he says. Points toward a group of people. We've still got our hands in our pockets and we both nod and move off.

I follow Dave up the steps into an apartment. People leaning against the stairway railing, nodding when we pass. Inside the apartment the air is clouded in thick smoke. Some brothers playing cards at a table just past the front door, Ben Moore, Chance McInnis, my brother's roommate, Wes Thompson. They all look up when we come in and my hands are shaking in my pockets. I ball them into tight fists.

Well look here, Ben says. He throws his cards against the table. It's the fucking golden boys.

Chance drops a cigarette into a beer can, props his elbows against the table, smiles and blows smoke from one corner of his mouth. Wes stands up and drapes an arm over my shoulder.

I was wondering when you'd get here, he says. I look up and his eyes are all red with the smoke.

Brett's out back, he says. Dave sits down beside Chance. He drops a hand on Dave's shoulder and Ben slides a bottle across the table. Dave grabs it just before it drops over the edge.

I'll walk you out, Wes says. I turn back and Dave doesn't look nervous at all and I'm wondering what bad things Chance used to tell him. Dave's smiling, bringing the beer up to his mouth. Ben and Chance grinning beside him. The narrow hallway crowded with people. When we pass the bathroom the door is cracked and there's a big guy sitting on the toilet and a girl with thin red hair straddling him, their mouths all tangled up. He's got his hands underneath her arms, moving her across his lap like she's a doll. He cracks an eye, sees me looking in, leans over with one thick arm and slams the door. In the kitchen three of my pledge brothers are talking. They've all got beers and when we pass by one points at me and nods seriously. This is all meant to mean yes, we are here, we did something good. I point back and he smiles.

Outside Brett is standing next to a keg, this blue hat pulled down over his eyes, talking to a short guy with long hair. He presses his hand down on a lever to pump beer from the keg. He laughs and looks up. Wes and I walk down the steps and Wes gets two plastic cups from beside the keg, holds the nozzle over one and begins to fill it. When it's full I reach for the cup but he hands it to a girl who's come up behind me.

Ladies first, he says and starts to fill the other cup. When he hands the next beer to me I raise it to my lips and pull out a cigarette. Brett lights it for me and we just stand there beside the keg pulling on our smokes. The short guy leaves and Brett nods toward him.

Later, he says.

I brought the man out to see you, Wes says, tilting his head over at me.

Yeah, Brett says. I was waiting on him to get here.

We're proud of you, Wes says. Real proud. Brett nods.

I'm pretty happy, I say. Scratch the back of my head.

No surprise, Wes says. You were a lock.

Nah, I say.

Damn straight you were, he says, and then I don't know what else to say about it because I am happy but at the same time everything seems off, somehow, like I don't belong here. Anywhere.

So, I'll leave you two to talk, Wes says. I got some shit to attend to. Back in there. He points toward the door.

Wes turns and hikes up the stairs back into the apartment. He looks back while he's holding the door and raises the red plastic cup into the air like a trophy. Asks Brett where he got the hat from. It says I Love Guam. Brett says he found it in a rickshaw in Charleston.

What? Wes says.

A rickshaw, Brett says. Rode in it.

Oh, Wes says. He turns, lets the door fall shut.

Dumbass, Brett says. Doesn't even know what a rickshaw is.

What're rickshaws doing in Charleston? I say.

Hippies pull them, he says. Cheaper than a taxi.

Brett bends the bill of his hat with both hands.

Fun, huh? Brett says. Looks around the backyard.

Yeah, it is, I say.

Fun fun fun, he says and I don't know what else to say.

Are you happy? he says.

Yeah. Sure. Really happy. I try to make it sound real. He looks at my face.

Nah. He shakes his head. You aren't.

Yes, I am, I say but I'm not even though I think I should be. I know somehow he's disappointed and I can't figure why this isn't good enough.

He's staring at me from beneath the hat and I can hear him thinking.

This is for you, all for you, because you are good enough, because you are my brother and you don't need me.

Brett has been keeping his distance the past week or so and I know it's because he wants me to do this alone. Because he wants me to know that I can do it.

He sprays beer into a cup. Eyes shaded by the baseball cap. He turns around in the yard and stares past the fence at the knotted trees. Walks toward a group of people gathered at the other apartment, stretches his arm out and flicks the cigarette toward the shrub. It flies like a bottle rocket and disappears in the shadows.

I KEEP DRINKING keg beer outside, talking but never really listening to people who wander out, looking over at Brett standing at another apartment talking to people there the way he won't talk to me. I keep wondering if he'll come back but he doesn't. He goes inside and I don't see him again.

Dave comes out after a while. Looks carefully at the steps walking down, pauses on the third step and takes a breath. He brushes the hair away from his face and it gleams in the over-head light. Comes down and starts filling his cup.

Whew, he says. His eyes are bloodshot. Gettin' drunk in there.

Yeah, I say. Me too.

He tilts his cup to keep the foam down. Why don't you come inside? he says.

I don't know, I say. It's nice out here.

Hot though.

Yep.

You're coming to the cabin though, right? It's part of this whole thing.

Sure. What time?

About an hour.

Come get me.

You sure you don't wanna come in?

Maybe in a minute.

Okay. He turns and takes the steps cautiously again.

After a few more minutes of waiting for Brett to come back I go inside and walk through all the people slouched against the walls. One girl with black hair smiles at me and I look at her for a moment, think it might be Michelle from the other night. She turns around and starts talking to another girl and I keep walking.

The beer has calmed my hands and I sit down next to Dave at the table with Ben and Chance and Wes. Wes has a girl sitting in his lap. She's holding a hand of cards and Wes keeps pointing to one. She giggles and drops one in a pile at the middle.

Drink, fucker, Wes says. He points at Ben. Drink you fat fuck, he says.

Ben stares across the table.

Fat? he says. He draws a circle on the table with his index finger. My dick's fat, he says. He lifts the beer to his mouth. Looks over at Wes again. Don't call me fat you bony bitch, he says.

Wes and the girl both laugh. Chance rubs his forehead and reaches over into my shirt pocket. Pulls out my cigarettes, shakes one into his mouth, drops them back into my pocket.

Thanks, he says.

It's nothing, I say.

Chance leans over to me. You remember how I said we'd get you some whores?

Yeah.

Well, you're in luck, son. There're plenty here. Plenty more at the cabin.

I nod. Good, I say. Good.

Chance laughs. I look down at my beer and start pulling at one end of the label and then I decide that I'm tired of feeling like something's not right so I drink until I finish the whole thing. Chance gives me another.

Damn, boy, he says. Thirsty? I nod and do the same with another beer.

I got just the thing for a thirsty pledge, he says. He reaches under the table and brings out a handle of Jim Beam. Unscrews the top and turns the heavy bottle up. His Adam's apple clicking up and down with the swallows. When he's done he wipes his mouth and pushes the bottle over toward me.

I want to impress him.

I want to be happy.

I want this all to be right.

The bottle warm in my hands. I run my nose over the top. The smell makes me wince and Chance laughs but I take the bottle and point the bottom straight toward the ceiling. Let my eyes roll back into my head. The swallows burn my throat but I keep going and when I'm done I slam the bottle down, squint my eyes hard and wipe my mouth. Chance looks at my face.

Hah, he says, that's how it's done. He grabs my shoulder and shakes me back and forth. I clutch his thick shoulder.

Hah, I say and we laugh for no reason and Chance crosses his arms in front of him on the table and lays his head between them. He pulls up all red-eyed, breathes in quickly and laughs again. I lean my chair back and it slips and I topple down beside the table. My face against the carpet and Chance stands and scoops me up beneath the arms like a baby and he laughs and everyone at the table laughs and I stand and hold my arms up like I've just won something and Ben pats me on the shoulder and Dave looks up at me and everyone starts clapping. I take a bow and sit back down. Pledges standing on the other side of the table clapping and smiling. My head starts to rock with the beer and the bourbon and the smoke and everything hums like it's all electric and I forget about Brett, forget about wanting him to be here with me in all the laughter and static and Ben slides the deck toward me and says it's my turn to deal.

I RIDE WITH Chance and Dave to the cabin. The whole way Chance's pulling from a silver flask with his initials on the front. He turns the radio up for this Kenny Loggins song "Danger Zone" from the movie *Top Gun*.

Damn, he says. Holds one hand flat against the air outside. I love that fucking movie.

Dave looks over at him flying his hand like an airplane. The air tosses Dave's hair all around his face.

Yeah, Dave says, all serious. All those fast airplanes and stuff.

I laugh. Chance looks at Dave and then turns around to me. What? he says.

Oh, I say. Nothing. Something from earlier. Chance looks back out the window, keeps flying his hand like it's an airplane. Dave turns around and rolls his eyes, twirls his finger around his head like Chance's crazy, and I nod.

Chance looks back at me and Dave.

What? Chance says. We can't stop laughing and Chance starts laughing too. He takes another pull from the flask and passes it back to me. I bring it up and it's stopped tasting bad, stopped tasting like anything.

We laugh again and the car drifts over the yellow line to the other side of the road. Chance takes the flask from Dave and when he's back on the right side of the yellow line he turns off the lights and we drive in the dark and he hangs his hand out again to split the air and there's nothing but the silent and warm darkness rushing inside.

THE DIRT PARKING lot at the cabin is choked with cars. It's a cinder-block building some rich alumni donated to the KA's, and they rent it out to other fraternities for parties and things. Chance pulls up and blocks two cars in and we don't say anything, we just get out and start walking and I hope my brother will be here and I think he will because everyone's supposed to, all the brothers, all the pledges. The gravel is loose and Dave slips once and then I slip right after that. Chance shakes his head at us.

You two know how to walk? he says.

Sure, I say and Dave laughs. Stumbles again. The voices coming from cars, from people slouched against them, the music from inside the cabin, it folds into this one thick hum. My contacts stick to my eyes. I rub them with two fingers, blink hard a few times. There's a line waiting to get in the front door and a big guy checking ID's so the fraternity won't be liable for underage drinking. He stands there all muscles and no neck, a shaved head, arms crossed in front of him between ID's. But it's just for show Chance tells us on the way there. No one really cares. All you have to do is show him something. It could say you're sixty-four and from Kalamazoo. Chance walks straight to the front of the line and Dave and I follow. The bouncer looks down at Chance and nods him in. When Dave walks by he puts a hand on his chest. Dave looks around like he doesn't know what to do and Chance walks up behind the big guy. Whispers in his ear. He takes the hand off Dave's chest and cocks his head toward the door.

INSIDE THERE'S AN eighties band onstage. Guys in their thirties. The lead singer has long, tightly curled hair. They start this song "Come On Eileen" right when we walk in and the crowd up front starts bouncing up and down. Chance leaves Dave and me, goes over to a crowd of girls. We get canned beers from plastic trash cans full of ice. They taste like water and Dave and I go into the crowd up front, duck below the raised arms and jumping cigarettes. Someone spills a beer down my arm. I look for Brett in the middle of all the jumping bodies. Wes is standing behind a girl, arms around her waist, twisting his crotch into her back. He holds his arms up and cheers when the chorus starts and his beer tips over onto the girl's head. She reaches up, pats her hair and keeps dancing. A pledge shuffles his feet and rocks his head. Another pledge sees us at the back of the crowd, holds an arm above all the heads and points. I point back and lead us toward Wes and I'm feeling all confident, pushing people aside and brushing past them like I'm someone who's supposed to be here, like this is for me. I grab Wes's shoulder and he turns around and smiles, raises his arms again and spills beer onto the girl's head again. I pat her head and she smiles. Turns back around and starts to dance, arms above her head. Wes doesn't say anything. Stands behind me and Dave, drops one hand on both our shoulders and screams, because, I guess, he's happy.

I lose count of the beers I've drunk somewhere around sixteen. A pledge leans into a corner of the room, head down against his chest. A girl tugs at his arm and he doesn't look up he just swats the hand away. Will Fitch stands next to the trash cans full of beer, stares straight ahead, blinks his eyes. The floor is slick with all the dirt from people's shoes mixing with spilled beer. The band stops playing at two-thirty. The lead singer brushes his greasy bangs away from his forehead and thanks everyone.

You guys know how to rock, he says. Balls one hand into a fist above his head. Everybody cheers, throwing arms up toward the ceiling. Rock and fucking roll, he says. My face feels numb. I sit down in a wooden chair in the middle of the cabin. Dave stands next to me, cocks a hip to the right and puts his hands in his back pockets and we're there in all the laughter and smoke and shifting bodies wondering why we were nervous at all because we're rock stars with our snarls and shirts drenched from the sweat and beer.

MY HEAD STARTS to drop to my chest and I can't keep my eyes open. A girl sits in my lap. I look up and she's there staring at my face. I don't recognize her but she seems to know me because she keeps saying I knew you'd get in, they had to have you. I give her a cigarette and put my hands around her hips. I can feel the edge where her jeans meet her stomach. I slide one hand around to the groove her spine makes down her back, run two fingers along it and she's looking at me and I'm looking at her with my numb face and she puts a palm flat against my chest, runs the hand down to my waist, turns around and pulls on the cigarette. Dave leans down to my ear.

Watch it, he says. I look up at him.

That's a brother's girlfriend, he says and I shrug like I don't care.

I'm serious, he says.

Fuck it, I say.

He shakes his head. You better hope nobody sees you, he says and I want to ask him if he's forgotten what we are, that we are rock stars, that right now we are gods. I keep my hands on the girl's hips, keep tracing the divot of her spine, the edge of her rib cage and then she's up and stumbling toward a big guy who's straining his neck to see all around the room. She puts her arms around his shoulders and he leans down and kisses her. Dave looks down at me.

Told you, he says.

Yeah, I say. Whatever. I get up and go for another beer. Will's still standing there beside the trash cans blinking his eyes.

Hey man, I say. He looks at me like mine is the first voice he's heard in a long time.

Oh, he says. What's up. I reach down into a trash can and all the ice is water. I pull my hand up and look at the others.

No beer, I say. Shake the water onto the floor. He keeps looking straight ahead and raises his arm toward me.

Here, he says. I don't want this anymore. He holds the beer out to me.

Thanks, I say. You sure? He nods and the beer is warm but my mouth is dry and I take the whole thing down in a few swallows. I crumple the can and throw it.

I saw you with that brother's girlfriend, he says.

Yeah, I say.

She's pretty, he says.

I couldn't really tell.

She is. He swivels his head around and looks at me.

Yeah, he says after a pause, she is. I remember to look for my brother but he's not anywhere. Will turns his head back toward the crowd like he's looking for someone. Everyone is slouching into one another full of the beer and the music and the room tilts and Will and I just stand there in the sway and rock of the bodies around us.

6

I N MY DORM room on Monday afternoon, waiting for the phone to ring, I keep thinking about what Brett said, that I had to make people like me, that it was the most important thing. I can't shake the feeling that I don't want to make anyone like me.

Pledge season officially starts when my phone rings. The brothers told us that we were going to a picnic with our little sisters, this group of sorority girls who do things with the fraternity. It's supposed to be a celebratory thing for pledges. My pledge brothers were excited when they heard this, said things like that's fucking cool of them, but for some reason I didn't buy it. I asked Brett about the picnic but he wouldn't elaborate, because it's this secret thing that he's not supposed to talk about. But I knew it wasn't going to be what the brothers told us because all Brett said was this: don't wear anything nice. I am wearing torn shorts, a green Velocity Girl T-shirt.

The shrill ring of the phone startles me away from my window and I jerk around, peer at the orange plastic rotary dial left over from the sixties. It shakes because the ring is so loud. On the second ring I take a step toward the phone. On the third I let my hand fall down close. On the fourth I force myself to pick it up.

Hello, I say.

Take your fucking goat ass to the hall right fucking now. The voice screaming. I can't tell who it is. The voice rattles a list of things I am to bring.

Two packs Marlboro Lights.

One *Hustler*.

A toothbrush.

I leave my dorm room, stumble down three flights of stairs, start toward the Cricket Mart. I pass through a brick arch that borders the soccer field, my feet crumpling scattered trash and dead leaves. Past the arch two brothers stand cross-armed leaning against a black truck. One winks as I turn and catch his glance. His lips pulled tight across gray teeth. The slight breeze tosses his red hair. I see two of my pledge brothers when I hit Main Street. Cars blaring music move slowly down the road, shirtless students hang from open windows. Dave Reed and Kevin Brehm look both ways, take a step and then jump back as a car blows its horn at them. Kevin punches Dave in the arm. They stumble into the road all smiles, laughing the whole way across. They see me standing. Gauging the traffic.

What's up, motherfucker? Kevin says. Slaps my back.

Nothing, I say. Look back and forth across the road again. In one hand Dave has Listerine, some Levi Garrett chewing tobacco. Two rolls of toilet paper, a magazine that I assume is porn tucked beneath his other arm. Kevin has everything in one hand, two packs of Camel cigarettes, a cheap disposable lighter. When I ask Kevin about the difference in their loads, he says fuck that, I ain't buying all that shit. Dave just nods his blond mop back and forth. It catches the light.

I told him he'd regret it, Dave says.

What the fuck are they going to do, beat the shit out of me? Kevin says. Fuck that. I'm fucking broke anyway. He looks back at a girl in a bikini top riding a bicycle. He smacks his lips and turns back to me.

This is pretty crazy shit, huh? he says. Guess we ain't going to no picnic. I nod. Dave says that they need to hurry and they shuffle off in the opposite direction. Drops his magazine and Kevin kicks him in the ass when he bends over to pick it up. I look back and see the two brothers still waiting by the black truck. When I cross the road I look over my shoulder again. One brother yanking things from Dave and Kevin. The other pushes Dave in the back as he and Kevin start toward the hall. Yells something I cannot make out.

I ONLY HAVE eight dollars and I don't want to blow it all so I only buy one pack of Marlboros and a toothbrush. The *Hustler* is seven dollars by itself. I really don't want to buy any of these things but the least I can do is get the brother with the gray teeth a toothbrush.

I have two dollars left and I crumple the bills and receipt into my pocket. When I open the double doors at the Cricket Mart I see across the road that the brothers are not waiting anymore and I think that maybe I will be the last pledge to show up at the hall.

I PUSH THE gray metal door open on the Kappa Sigma hall and see Dixon Lynch and Patrick Wells. Patrick is short and thick. Wearing sunglasses. Trying to make himself look like a badass. He's yelling at Will Fitch, who's taller than he is. He points up toward Will, pokes his stubby ring finger back and forth inches from his face. Will flinches each time. Patrick yells. Flails his arms. Tries to look his meanest. Dixon just smirks. His face is dark with stubble. He pushes Will toward the short stairwell that leads up into the hall. Will catches a foot on the first step, stumbles and then rights himself. Looks back at Dixon, who says that if he looks back again he'll break his fucking face. Patrick sees me standing with my back to the door. It almost makes me wince to see him turn so quickly toward me, his eyebrows rising, his lip curling slightly. My hands are shaking. I smile. Try to hide the fact that I'm scared. Patrick grabs the front of my T-shirt and pulls me away from the door.

What the fuck are you smiling for? he says. He stares hard at me. I look away.

Huh? he says, cups a palm beneath my chin, spins my head around to face him.

I'm fucking talking to you, he says. I said what the fuck are you smiling for? Dixon comes from my right and slaps the glasses from my face. They spin across the floor and rest beside a trash can.

Take those fucking glasses off, he says. Everything blurs, Patrick and Dixon's faces, the walls, the light streaming from outside. Patrick says that I am fucking pathetic. His breath hot on my face and it makes me wince. Dixon takes the cigarettes and the toothbrush I'm holding, pulls them from my clenched hand, stuffs the toothbrush into his back pocket like a comb. Patrick moves behind me. Places his hands on my shoulders. Pushes me up three steps. The door leading into the hallway is closed but through it I hear muffled voices. A brother waiting on me at the top of the stairs. He is much taller and much bigger than I am. I feel Patrick's hands leave my shoulders. The brother at the top of the stairs looks at me. His face scarred from acne, his skin rough from the beginnings of a beard. He does not yell. He does not poke his finger toward me.

When you walk in there, he says, pointing toward the closed door and leaning down, I want you to yell. And what I want you to yell is that you own this fraternity. I mean it. He pauses. Looks at me sincerely.

I want you to look at everyone and scream at the top of your lungs. This is your fraternity. You own it.

I place my hands on the door and push.

THERE IS A line of brothers down each side of the hallway and pledges are filing between them. Will somewhere halfway down. A brother pushes him in the back. He spins limply toward the opposite wall, where Chance meets him with another shove. I wonder where Brett is. His door is shut and a brother is leaning against it. Everyone yelling. I throw my hands up. For a moment I can't remember what I am supposed to say but when a brother catches my eye I remember, say that I own this fraternity. At first it comes out softly but then I see the anger welling up in the brother's eyes. He clenches his face and then I am screaming, flailing my arms, bouncing toward the gauntlet like a madman.

I own this motherfucker, I say. A brother grabs me. Jerks me by one arm. I am still screaming.

What the fuck did you say? he says. You fucking goat motherfucker I'm gonna fuck you up if you say that again. I do not look at him I just scream. Chance hears me. Another brother's head spins around after he shoves Will and now all eyes are on me. A brother flings me down the line and now I am being thrown from side to side. My body goes limp and I just let the shoves come. I reach the end of the line. A brother opens the door to the hall lounge and pushes me inside. The door slams behind me. I am still screaming that I own the fraternity. There are composite pictures lining the walls. A large star painted on the back wall. It contains the Greek letters kappa and sigma and a crescent moon with a skull in the middle. Two crossed swords border the star on each side. The star and moon painted in green and red. A television on one wall. Trophies line a cabinet. A pool table in the middle of the room. The brother who is the pledge master grabs me when he hears what I'm saying. He's big, six-five, and he talks slowly even though he's trying to sound furious.

Shut your fucking hole, he says, like his mouth is full of novocaine. He puts one large hand behind my neck, his fingers resting against my ears. It feels as if he's going to hoist me up like a dog hauls her young.

Get on the goddamn floor with your pledge brothers, he says. Shoves me down. I land on my knees, behind the line of pledges sitting cross-legged, their heads bowed toward their legs, their arms locked tightly together. They bob like the pistons of an engine. They are bahing like goats. The sound rises and falls. It fills the room.

I lock arms with Will.

Bah like a goat, motherfucker, someone says.

We bah.

Louder, he says. We bah louder. I push my head closer to my legs. Sweat is pouring down my back and my arms are slick.

Get down, faggot, a brother says. Someone is shoved down next to me. Through a squinted eye I see Dave Reed and his shaggy blond hair. Dave locks arms with me tightly. Someone yanks at Dave's arm.

You better fucking hold on, faggot, a voice says. I better not be able to tear you off. I am holding tightly but Dave's arm slips through mine. I will not look up. Dave disappears and then slams back down next to me, sends me teetering into Will and we pull the whole line backward.

Bah, we say.

Bah bah bah.

I feel spit hit the back of my neck. It rolls down into my shirt warm, slips down my back slowly. Someone whispers in my ear. It is soft almost gentle and I can feel hot breath against the side of my face like someone is bending to kiss my cheek.

I fucking hate you, he says, you hear me? I hate every single one of you goat motherfuckers. A hand slaps the back of my head. At each end brothers pull the line, try to loosen us.

Hold on, motherfuckers, you better fucking hold on, someone says. Everything is beginning to blend together and everything sounds like a chant, the goat sounds, the yelling, the sway of the line. Will crying next to me. I can hear him whimpering. I cannot cry. I squeeze my knees around my head until it hurts.

GET UP, A brother says. We all rise, heads bowed. Stand clustered together. The whole room still rings. My arms are stiff, my legs throb and my body is soaked in sweat and spit and there's Vaseline in my hair. Dave has toothpaste in his hair. Will's hair glistens and it's slicked down in the back. He smells like flowers. Ben Moore dumped Summer's Eve on his head. Another pledge is missing one sleeve from his blue oxford button-down, his brown belt fastened around his neck like a noose. Two other pledges, twins, have red splotched faces. Handprints on their cheeks. Eyes bloodshot. Another pledge standing dazed. Squints his eyes tightly. His glasses have been taken. He cannot see.

Another brother lines us up.

Nothing happened, right? he says. We nod. Dixon and Patrick come in. Patrick takes my arm. We walk through an open door and he whispers in my ear.

Just a little more, okay? he says. You're doing good. Just a little more. He pulls me into the courtyard. The lucid sunlight. I squint my eyes at the glare and brush my hair back from my forehead. The pledges are walking single file. A few brothers walking beside us. Dave in front of me, the blue clumps of toothpaste forming knots, his hair like a bird's nest. Chance leans in close to his ear. Dave nods and keeps his eyes on the ground. We pile down concrete stairs that lead to the dorm parking lot. It is five spaces wide. Eight cars have pulled in. Five in spaces, three on the grass. I see a brother standing beside a two-door red Corolla. He's smoking, thick black hair pulled in a sweep across his forehead, his pink skin beaming in the afternoon light. Another brother sitting on the trunk dangling his legs back and forth. Everyone is pushed toward a car. One pledge gets into the back of the red Corolla. Patrick ducks my head and pushes me into the center of the backseat. Kevin Brehm gets in behind me. Patrick leans in when Kevin sits down.

Keep your heads down, he says. Places one hand on each side of the doorframe. He smiles, winks at me, slams the door and then he is gone.

My back is arched and it hurts to bend down so I keep my head raised. I look at the pledge on my left. Staring through the window. On my other side, Kevin is slapping his knees. Nursing this beat. Bobbing his head. The pledge on my left looks at him.

What the fuck are you doing? he says. He was a model in New York before he came to Clemson. Brett told me that even though he's a Yankee they let him in because he's a bitch magnet. Because he can pull ass. Kevin turns his head slowly toward the model pledge. Drums his knees.

I don't know, Kevin says. Just fucking around I guess.

Well fucking quit, he says. I don't wanna see you bop your skinny fucking neck. Kevin stops slapping his knees. The model pledge turns back toward the window.

Jesus, the pledge says. Rubs his stubbled chin. You think they'd turn on the fucking air-conditioning. Sweat streaming down his forehead. Wearing a yellow Juicy Fruit T-shirt. A large wet spot spread across his chest.

Why would you think that? I say and he just squints at me and shakes his head.

You're right, he says, turning again toward the window. Why

would I think these assholes would turn on the AC? I don't know. Decency. Something like that.

I wipe my forehead with the bottom of my T-shirt. The driver's side door opens and a brother gets in.

This brother drinks bourbon in biology class. He gets a Coke in a plastic bottle, pours out half, fills it back up with Jim Beam. His eyes always bloodshot. The first thing he ever asked me was if I liked to eat pussy. You cannot trust a man who doesn't like to eat pussy, he said. I said, yes, I like to eat pussy. He smiled. Licked his teeth. He is from Sumter, South Carolina. His favorite things are eating pussy and drinking bourbon. Another brother gets in the passenger seat. He is from Hartsville, South Carolina. He turns around.

Whew, he says, fanning himself. It's fucking hot in here. You goat fuckers hot?

The other brother laughs. They are both sweating but they won't turn on the air-conditioning. Instead they leave the windows down. One brother cranks the car and slides it into gear. We back out of the parking lot. The brother has one arm behind the passenger seat, looking backward. He pulls out in front of an approaching Jeep. Throws up his middle finger as he turns around.

Fuck off, he says.

Keep your heads down and bah, the other brother says. We put our heads between our legs and bah.

Louder, he says.

We bah louder. The air streams in from outside and it feels good against the back of my head. Through my crossed arms I catch Kevin's eye. He is smiling. I turn back toward the floor.

Are you boys ready to fuck a goat? the brother that's driving says. I'm glad I don't ever have to do that again. It don't feel good. But you better get ready 'cause right here in a minute that's what you're gonna be doing. Fuck fuck fucking a goat, he says, breaking into song. Laughing.

Bah, motherfuckers, the other one says. Pulls his knees up onto the seat and turns around, perches like a hawk, pushes his neck forward when he yells.

Bah bah bah, he says. We're in the car for fifteen minutes and the whole time I am bahing and wondering if we are really going to have to fuck a goat.

GRAVEL CRUNCHES UNDER the tires and we stop.

The brothers roll up the windows and get out. One leans back in just as he is about to shut the door.

Don't move, he says. Keep your heads down and stay bahing real loud. I wanna be able to hear you through the car. He slams the door. Even though it's late afternoon it's very hot. The sun shines through the windows and cooks the air inside. It hurts to breathe. We're bunched together tightly. Legs and arms sweating against one another. Too afraid to look up. Under his breath I can hear the pledge from New York saying over and over that this is so fucked up and if one person touches him again he is going to kill them. I pray silently, furiously, that he will and that this will be over. The passenger side door opens and Kevin is yanked out. He whimpers and his foot brushes my knee. The door slams again and the model pledge and I are alone with the sweat and the thick air.

When the door opens again the air rushes in from outside. I feel a mouth press close to my ear.

What's my name? someone says. I recognize the voice. It's Chance. His breath in my ear.

Chance, I say. I don't look up.

Don't say my fucking name, he bawls. Then he's gone. Another voice presses close to my ear.

His name is piece of shit fuckface, the new voice says. I try to place it but cannot. When he asks you better fucking say it. As quickly as he was gone Chance is back again.

What's my fucking name? he says. I pause for a moment. Let out a long breath.

Piece of shit fuckface, I say. A closed fist lands on the back of my head and makes my ears ring. My head throbs with the heat and the fist. Three more times.

What's my name?

Chance. Wrong. Closed fist.

What's my name?

Mr. McInnis. Wrong. Closed fist.

What's my name?

Mr. Piece of Shit Fuckface. Wrong. Closed fist.

Nothing works. I'm pulled from the car. I glance up quickly. There's a cabin in front of me. Surrounded by thick woods and I don't know where I am. Its gray cinder-block sides and black shingled roof gleam in the retreating light. Cars parked all around. Chance drags me by my arm and my feet scuff the ground. I look back down at the grass, the speckled dirt path that leads to the cabin. Chance shoulders me inside. It's dark. I look around. The only light comes from one open door and two windows coated in a brown film. Groups of brothers stand against the cinder-block walls of the room. A small bar on the far wall. A stage at the front. The floor is wet and sticks to my shoes. Everywhere my pledge brothers are screaming like goats.

They are shoved against walls.

They are writhing on the ground.

Ben Moore grabs me. Throws me against the wall.

Fuck the wall, he says.

I fuck the wall.

Fuck the floor, he says.

I fuck the floor. I am passed to Patrick Wells and thrown against another wall. I throw my forearms in front of me and they split open on the rough cinder block. I have to fuck the wall again. Patrick is laughing. His hands on my waist. Shoves my hips into the wall again and again.

Come on, goat, he says, fuck that wall.

I am passed to the bar. A pledge on top. Fucking the bar. Dixon tells me to fuck my pledge brother. I climb up but another brother sees me. His coal-black hair wet around the edges from sweat. Thick curls stick to his forehead and he looks tired. He pulls me off and says to sit down, that he doesn't want to see two pledges fucking. Dave Reed sitting with his head bowed. His shirt torn, one knee is busted open. A rose-colored bruise forming on his left shin.

THE PLEDGE CLASS sits on the edge of the three-foot-high stage at the front of the cabin, feet dangling over the edge. The room still vibrates from all the screaming and I can see the light growing fainter through the one open door. Dave Reed on my left and Will Fitch on my right. A brother shoves a bottle into my hand. The glass scalding hot because someone's heated it up and I can barely keep my fingers wrapped around it. I clasp it lightly with my fingertips. A crowd of brothers is in front of us. I look for Brett standing among them but cannot find him. We play a game.

One brother asks a question and points to a pledge. The pledge answers and it is wrong. We drink the heated-up beer without stopping and it burns our throats. This is how it goes:

Question.

Answer.

Wrong.

Drink.

After the third beer I feel as if I am going to vomit. I look to my left. Dave Reed doubled over retching onto the floor. It splashes on a brother's shoe.

Fuck me, the brother says. Looking down in bewilderment. He raises his foot from the ground. Gives Dave another beer. He begins to drink but pukes again. When a brother gives me another beer I raise it to my lips. I look for Brett again and see him standing at the back of the room ten feet away from the crowd. His arms crossed, he glares right at me. He doesn't do anything. He just stares, his brown eyes hollow. But I want him to see that I am strong, that he did this once and now I am doing it. I tilt my head up to drink and let the beer stream down from my mouth onto my shirt because I know that I will puke if I take another sip. No one notices because my shirt is already soaked and everyone is yelling and puking. My head is spinning and when I look back toward Brett he is gone.

THE PLEDGE CLASS goes outside and the brothers pat us on the back. Patrick Wells tells me good job, I did good. Chance slaps my back with his meaty hands. My muscles have already begun to tighten. My left calf jerks in a fit, clenches itself, loosens when I reach down to grab it. Brothers are taking pledges back to campus. I'm looking for someone to ride with. I see Brett waiting beside his car, one leg crossed over the other. The insects have begun their late-afternoon whine and when he sees me walking toward him he opens his door and gets in, one arm hanging from the window, smoke from his cigarette curling over the car's roof.

When I get into Brett's car he tells me that what I just did is the worst part. He doesn't look at me. They do it to weed out the weak ones, he says. We're driving back and the outside air cools my face. The sun is dipping below the edge of Lake Hartwell, spilling shadows across the dam, and my brother is staring at something out in front of him.

7

THE RADIO STATION plays a country song. I switch it off, push the white sheets back and place my feet on the floor. The television is still on, spilling light through the room. A bald man wearing a gray suit is pointing at a map of the United States, following weather systems with an open hand. I rub my eyes, move my shoulder around to work out the stiffness. I raise one arm, touch the wound from where I hit the wall yesterday. It's soft and gummy. Almost black. Same on the other forearm. Didn't leave any blood on the sheets though. I cross my arms over my chest, shiver from the cold. The air-conditioning in the dorm rooms is always either too hot or too cold. My roommate sleeps in his raised loft and his clothes hang from the foot of his bed. I put on my flip-flops and open the door. Click the large bolt down quietly when I am in the hall so as not to wake my roommate. The shower room at the end of the hall. A large black trash can on both ends. Pizza boxes flat across each one's top, trash collected in corners behind them. A single blue stripe painted in the center of each cream-colored wall. It stops when it meets a door and then starts again until it meets another. My towel is around my waist and it is six-fifteen and feels like the world will never wake up.

FOR THE FIRST week of pledge season the class must meet for breakfast every day at seven o'clock. This is to create unity. I have risen so early because I do not want to be late. Our pledge master says it's imperative to be on time. It will be very bad if someone doesn't show up at all. If one person messes up we all have to eat breakfast together for another week.

It is still dark outside. Fine mist falling in the early morning. I'm wearing a blue blazer, white shirt, a red striped tie because all the pledges have to wear a coat and tie to breakfast. The rain stands in beads on my coat. My shoes splash in water on the path to the cafeteria. I look at the watch my father gave me. The brown leather band worn, frayed around the face. I still have ten minutes and I miss my father and wish he were here to tell me everything is okay, but he isn't, and even if he were here everything would still be fucked up.

I CLIMB THE white concrete stairs to Harcombe Dining Hall and move under the awning to escape the rain. The cafeteria isn't even open yet. In front of me safety lamps light the court-yard and I look at the mist falling through the light and it feels like the saddest I have ever been.

I look around for someone. Something to stare at besides the dark and the rain. I crouch in a corner beside the cafeteria's front double doors, cover my face with open palms and feel like I might cry. My arms hurt. I wrapped toilet paper around the cuts but you can't see it because of my jacket. I look to my right, see a foot move forward, a leg stretch from the shadow. Will Fitch steps out of the dark like a ghost.

Pretty early, huh? he says, placing his hands in his pockets. He's always shuffling through his pockets.

Yeah, I say. I am glad to see someone but I don't want to talk. Will stands next to me rigidly, fumbles through his pockets, pushes his green tie up into the collar of his blue shirt and I slump against the outside of Harcombe, and it feels good to see Will, to know that someone else has to look at the dark and the rain. We don't say anything else. We watch the rain fall and we wait for the lights in the cafeteria to come on and a door to open.

I GET THE pledge manual on a Tuesday. It's called the *Bononia Docet*. It's green with gold letters. Ben Moore tells me it's my Bible. Throw the other one out, he says. This is the only one that matters.

I start looking it over in my room. There are all these passages underlined in pencil.

The first one I read is this list of different rules for making people feel comfortable during rush.

The fifth rule says this:

5. Keep in mind what you are selling. You are selling a group of
   friends who are not only diverse and varied in interest, but who
   share the same values.

A few pages later, the book talks about official things like colors, which are emerald green, white and scarlet red, and how it's okay to call the Kappa Sigma Fraternity (its official name) Kappa Sig.

I read about how things like good taste and manners are very important. Then I read about the best ways to introduce people and how to shake hands.

After that, the book says this:

> Hazing is fundamentally at odds with the ideals of Kappa Sigma. Hazing runs contrary to all our concepts of brotherhood development. Under the Rules of the Kappa Sigma Fraternity, every chapter prohibits hazing in all forms within its own chapter bylaws. Your Supreme Executive Committee has adopted the following definition of hazing:
>
> Hazing is defined as any action taken or situation created, whether on or off Fraternity premises, by any Kappa Sigma chapter or by any Kappa Sigma member, to produce or result in mental or physical discomfort, embarrassment, harassment, or ridicule. Such activities would include paddling or physical abuse in any form, creation of excessive fatigue, physical or psychological shocks, involuntary road trips or any other activities which may tend to expose initiates or pledges to physical danger, morally degrading or humiliating games and activities, any activities which would disrupt public order or tend to bring the Fraternity into disrepute in the local community, and any other activities which are not consistent with Kappa Sigma Fraternity law.

I close the book with the rules in my head and I can't stop thinking about all of it. I have to slap myself hard before I can go to sleep.

WILL FITCH REACHES for the door to the Kappa Sigma hall like he's entering a morgue. His hand trembles and he's moving slow toward the handle. I stand behind him and glance from side to side. I am gun shy. Looking over my shoulder every second or two.

Just do it, I say. Just grab it and pull. I rattle change around in my pocket. He turns around. Looks at me like I don't know what I'm talking about, and he's right, I don't. I'm as scared as he is. I know what's on the other side.

It's six o'clock on a Tuesday and hot even though the sun is fading, dipping behind the burnt oaks and the football stadium that stands behind Daniel Hall.

Dude, just open it, I say.

Man, he says, fucking hold on. His hands shaking. I'm trying to get straight.

All right, I say, all right. Take your time.

Will turns and pushes the silver bar with the butt of one shaking palm and the cool air from inside smacks our faces.

EACH WEEKNIGHT TWO pledges have to go to every brother's room on the first, second and third floors, and ask if they need anything whatsoever. It's called a hall check. Will and I are the first two pledges to go.

I'm surprised when we move through the double doors to find no one waiting for us. I expect to hear screams because the last time we were standing here we were getting run through a gauntlet. Getting the shit kicked out of us. I look around, place one hand on the chipped black railing and look up to check the stairwell. Will is reaching for the second set of double doors that lead to the first floor.

What are you doing? he says.

I look back to him. Just checking, I say.

He shuffles his feet. See anyone? he says.

No, I say, it's clear. I glance back up one more time. Will pushes the door open and when we step onto the first floor my feet make a scraping noise. I look down and see that I've left two footprints. The floors on the hall are coated with dirt. One bathroom stands at the end of each floor and is shared by eighteen people.

Will stares into the first door on our left. He turns back, gives me this look like he's wondering what I'm doing standing back and letting him take the frontline. Somewhere a television blares but no one is home. The only other sound is from a stereo faintly playing a Bob Marley tune somewhere down the hall. Everyone leaves doors open on the hall because it's supposed to make us feel welcome but Will and I know better. I look at my footprints again and now there are six and I feel like a coward for letting Will and his trembling hands take the first steps.

MY BROTHER'S ROOM is next. I don't expect him to want anything but what do I know, my brother has been as much a mystery to me as anything else. Because I expected Brett to be my guide, to tell me what's what, and even though he's told me a few things, given me warnings, I feel like he's left me alone. And I know he wants me to make a go by myself, but I also know he feels strange about it all, like this fraternity isn't what he thought it was in the beginning, like he's not who he used to be, like once he saw it happening to me it was all different.

Will stays behind me this time. Brett is sitting on a rust-colored couch. Feet propped on a chipped coffee table strewn with cigarettes and beer cans. He's watching television. *Magnum, P.I.* I'm apprehensive even in my brother's room. He sees us and sits up quickly.

Come in, he says. You okay?

Yeah, I say. Look down at the gray industrial carpet. I turn back up and Brett is studying my face. He always does this when he thinks I'm lying and I am lying now and he knows it. Will steps into the room. Brett doesn't even look at him.

Do you need anything? Will says. We're making the hall check. Brett is still staring at me. He knows I don't like this. He knows it scares me. And I think he wants me to say it. To be honest. To say I'm scared. To say that it's fucked up. Because part of him, I know, feels the same way.

He breaks his stare and turns to Will.

No. No. Nothing, he says. Slouches back into the couch. He changes the channel and we leave.

Outside Brett's room there's a bulletin board. A list for in-tramural soccer, a clipping about a chapter in Georgia doing something charitable. Near the bottom a picture cut from a magazine of a woman with a penis. It says 1-900-SHE-MALE. The breasts are large and she's cupping one breast with one hand and squeezing the penis with the other. Someone has taken a photograph and cut out Dixon's head and taped it over the she-man's head. Dixon's head is large and doesn't fit the body. Above the doctored picture is a T-shirt. Pinned up with tacks, stretched out at the sleeves and neck. A dark brown patch covering the front and small red specks about the sleeves and collar. Someone has fastened a scrap of light green paper above the shirt and scribbled Dixon on it. I put my head around the corner of Brett's door.

What's the T-shirt? I say. Brett still on the couch.

Oh, he says, Dixon Lynch did that. Broke a cue over some kid's head last night. That's his T-shirt.

The kid's?

No. Dixon's.

Whose blood is it?

Both I think. Mostly the kid, though.

I leave Brett with his cigarettes and the television and look one more time at the bloodstained T-shirt and it reminds me of an ink blot test but I can't make anything out of the stains and the flecks. It's all just blood.

BEN MOORE WANTS an egg roll. I hate Ben Moore. He wants a pack of Marlboros and an egg roll. He's just in the mood, he says, and it must be from China Garden because they have the best egg rolls. It doesn't matter that the restaurant is five miles from campus. Chance wants his girlfriend's car pitted because he says he's about to get some. Pitting a car means driving it to a parking lot called the pit, a huge lot about a mile from campus. Parking is scarce on campus so most students have to park their cars in the pit. Will and I don't have cars anywhere near our dorms (both are in the pit) so for us pitting a car means driving the brother's car to the pit, parking and walking the mile back to our dorms. We take Chance's car to get the cigarettes and the egg roll and I keep the receipts. If we didn't have Chance's car, we'd have to walk. We drive past the football stadium down the road that dips and curves to the pit. It's eight o'clock, somewhat dark outside, still hot. I can feel the heat coming off the black tar as we walk the slope behind the stadium. I'm sweating and my shirt and hair are drenched. My glasses slide down the bridge of my nose. Will is worried that the egg roll will be cold, that we'll have to go get another. I say I'll stick the egg roll up Ben Moore's fat ass before I'll go get another but we both know I won't do anything like that.

I OPEN BEN'S door sweating and the silver knob slips between my fingers. I wipe my hands on my shirt and try again. Grease has seeped through the egg roll's white wrapping. Ben is still in his room. The television bounces off his glasses. I step inside and Will follows quietly behind. I give Ben the cigarettes and the egg roll. He thumps the Marlboros into an open palm, chokes the tobacco down close to the filter. He opens the pack and Dave and I stand motionless waiting for something to happen. Ben looks up. Cigarette dangling from his lips. Hands cupped. One thumb perched on a pink lighter.

What? he says. You can leave. He swats us away with one hand like we're insects. I hear the egg roll fall with a thud into his metal wastebasket.

ON THE SECOND floor Will sweeps Patrick Wells's room and I fold his newly washed clothes.

Get up there, goat, Patrick says, and I look up from the

clothes and see Will standing on a chair beside the wardrobe. He puts his feet on Patrick's shoulders, climbs up into the top five-by-three-foot compartment, and it takes a minute, Will's legs out over the front, bent over with his chest almost touching his thighs, he has to twist himself to fit. When Will's inside, his back touches the top, his head's between his legs, he looks like a folded piece of paper. Patrick laughs because it is funny to see Will all mashed up seven feet from the floor. He looks around and tries to find something to make me do and when he can't, he turns up to Will, says fuck it get down, goat, and see if anybody else needs you two fucks. Will throws his legs over the side of the compartment and puts his feet on my shoulders. He wobbles trying to squeeze himself out, twists until he can jump down. Patrick tells us to get the fuck out of his room because he has to study. No one else on the second floor needs anything and Will and I feel like we came out lucky.

ON THE THIRD floor we wash out seven plastic Miller Lite cups filled with tobacco spit in the bathroom sinks. There are three sinks. Will uses the sink on the far right and I use the middle one. The brother gives us Dawn to make the suds. The bathroom always reeks. The dark brown spit clumps in the sink, the water does not drain and the spit and tobacco all swirl around with hair. I gag from the smell. I leave the middle sink and move to the far left sink. Will says gross, that's really gross, and I know I have to reach through the water and unclog the hair and the spit because someone will ream me if I don't. I shove my hand into the water and feel for the drain, pull the hair out and run to the toilet to throw it in. I fling the blue door open, lean in and the hair splashes in the water. I turn around and see myself in the long mirror above the sinks. What are you doing? I ask myself. Shake my head back and forth. I stand crouched over with my hands on my knees and tell myself to breathe. Will has suds up to his elbows and he asks me what's wrong. I just look at him. A brother comes in with four plates and some forks all dried with food. Tells us while we're at it, why don't we just go ahead and wash these too. He looks into the drained middle sink. There is still tobacco lining the edges.

You better wash that shit down, he says. Points. Looks at himself in the mirror, brushes his red hair with a black plastic comb and leans forward. He presses two fingers against his cheek and mashes a pimple. Fuck, he says, looking at the blood he's left on his hands. He takes some toilet paper and blots his face on his way out.

THE CUPS ARE clean and dry when we bring them back to the brother. He says good work, goats, takes the top cup from the stack and spits tobacco over the lip. It streaks brown the whole way down and the brother tells us to leave, that he appreciates it mightily. There's only one other brother at home on the third floor and he's studying so he doesn't want anything.

WE LEAVE DANIEL HALL tired and filthy from the work, stumble into the thick air and Will turns, looks at me and breathes a long sigh. Places his hands on his slim hips and says that Ben Moore is a real bastard. I nod.

Fuck him, I say.

Yeah, Will says. Fuck him. He's a shitfuck.

What?

Shitfuck. Nothing. Nevermind.

I look at him and grin, give a feeble wave of my hand and turn to go up to my room.

That night I dream of shadows. Nothing coherent, just this darkness at the doors and windows. I wake up sweating, still dirty from the hall check. Heart pounding. Go over to the window and check to see if it's shut. Check the door lock. The television flashing. I sit on my bed and stare at the colors and I know then that it was the smile and the breath I was dreaming about. Or brothers. Whichever. But it doesn't really matter. They're the same thing.

I wait for sunlight before I sleep.

IT'S MY SECOND week and the fraternity owns me. The brothers are everywhere, waiting for me to slip. I walk to class and look for brothers. I eat and look for brothers. I'm in my room waiting on the phone to ring or for a fist to pound on my door. I sleep and now the smile and the breath are always in my dreams, dark and faceless, screaming, leering down at me and I am a quivering breathless child.

Late in the afternoon I dress in a navy blue sport coat (the only one I own), a white oxford shirt that fits loosely on my shoulders, a red tie and brown loafers. This is what we're supposed to wear. Personal appearance is important. The pledge master tells us that he doesn't want to see any fucking sloppy pledges and that brown shoes are correct, white or blue shirts are correct, solid or striped ties are correct, but, above all, he doesn't want to see any jeans or shorts or hats or any other weird shit because those are for Yankee fucks and faggots. We wear these things like we are soldiers, like they are holy, like we have never known any other clothes before.

I LEAVE MY room at six o'clock and hurry over to Tillman Hall. Tillman is the most recognizable spot on campus. Its clock tower looks over the burnt-orange brick buildings and can be seen from any point on campus. It rings out the hours in dull one-note clangs. I climb the stairs to the second floor and find room two sixteen. I have the number scribbled on my palm. Most of my pledge brothers are standing around nervously, still wary of any place we are told to gather. The air inside the room heavy like an old church. Dust moves through the room's muffled light like tiny dancing cells and every time I step on the faded green carpet clouds sprout behind my feet. Portraits of old men with white hair and black robes line the walls. They surround us, each of them austere and brilliant, their eyes fixed on every person here and we cannot move, we cannot breathe without someone watching us.

Will Fitch stands by himself behind the other fifteen pledges, pacing around a brown wooden chair. Eyes fixed on the floor. His blue shirt is wrinkled and his tie dangles loosely from the buttoned collar. His cheeks glow like he's been facing a stiff wind. I sit down in the chair and he continues to pace around me. He doesn't look up.

So, I say. Are you okay, man? He keeps walking. The circles become wider. He shrugs his shoulders.

Yeah, he says, brings a hand to his head, weaves fingers through thick blond hair. I'm just, I don't know, this is hard. I feel weird.

I don't know what to say. I want to tell him that I feel weird too, that my stomach is in knots but I just watch him pace and say nothing. I cross my arms over my chest. Dave Reed talking quietly to another pledge. Everyone speaking in hushed tones. Like we are in the presence of something holy. It fills the room in a low hum.

Patrick Wells enters the room from a door directly in front of me between two glaring old men. The door falls shut behind him and he just stands there looking at us. Everyone turns to face him. Our hands fall to our fronts, palms laid flat over each other, and we are standing and breathing the heavy air, waiting for his mouth to open and for words to part the silent room.

Patrick leads us into a large white room. Sunlight streams through the tall windows, lands in shafts on the floor. A crowd of brothers stands at the back and they follow us with their eyes, thirty heads turning at once. The pledge master is standing at the front of the room underneath a large portrait of an old man. White hair pulled back. Black robe. Mouth in a slit. A gold plate beneath the picture says Thomas Green Clemson. He was the founder of the university. The look on his face says it all. That this is sacred. There is a pulpit directly below the portrait with what looks like a Bible laid open. Will in front of me. Every so often I see his right hand twitch at his side. We march in, all seventeen pledges, until Patrick stops the line and we turn to face the front. I can feel the brothers' stares and I wonder if Brett is there burning holes in our backs like everyone else. I do not listen when the pledge master begins to talk.

The air is pulsing and I know that I should be listening solemnly but all I can think of is how the words mean nothing, that somehow this is all wrong.

All of the pledges bend down to one knee and huddle shoulder to shoulder in a circle. There's an open Bible on the floor in the middle of us, and we all place our hands together on top of it. Our eyes closed, the Bible underneath all the sweaty palms. We swear allegiance to God and Kappa Sigma and I crack one eyelid slightly even though I know someone might see. Will mouths the words, his dry lips shift against each other awkwardly like he can't keep up. His eyes flutter.

I close my eyes again and move my lips like I mean every word.

The pledge class says amen and stands. We all turn around at the same time and face the brothers at the back of the room. The brothers clap, all smiles. One by one a brother takes a pledge aside and sticks a pin onto his lapel. No one comes for me and Brett is nowhere. My pledge brothers spread away from me and at the end I am the only one standing, looking from face to face, at the ground, at anything to break the awkwardness of standing alone in the center of a room. Patrick Wells touches Dave Reed on the back and I see Dave jerk then smile. Patrick comes over and pulls me aside.

Listen, Robert Tinsley, he's your big brother, he couldn't make it today, class or something, so I'm gonna pin you, he says. I don't even know Robert Tinsley, and can't figure out why someone who knows me isn't my big brother. Patrick's meaty hands fish around through his jacket and he pulls out a pin, pulls my right lapel forward a bit and weaves the pin through the thick navy blue cloth. Pats it gently with an open palm, looks me over and says that it looks damn good on me. I look down, rub the pin softly with my thumb. It is so small. I look for Brett again. I look at Patrick.

Where's Brett? I say.

You know him, he says. He does what he wants to. I guess he didn't want to come.

I nod. And then I squint through the bent shaft of light that is still heating my face and shoulders, look out the window, trying to find my dorm but everything is white and dense and I can't make it past the windowsill.

EVERYONE BUT WILL FITCH is gone when I step outside of Tillman into the late afternoon. He's sitting on the front steps. Loosening his tie. I plop down next to him. He looks at me and nods.

Who's your big brother? I say.

Chance McInnis, he says. Still looking straight ahead. I nod and he doesn't say anything back.

Mine wasn't here today, I say. Class or something.

Will picks up a leaf from beneath his feet. Starts tearing one side. Picks at the leaf delicately like he's performing surgery and I see his right hand twitch again. He holds the leaf in his left hand and shakes his right one a few times. I don't say anything about the twitching. I just figure if he wanted to he'd tell me. The sun, a tangerine slit on the horizon, looks like it's being stretched on both sides. It spills over the small hills behind Lake Hartwell, casting long shadows, and everything seems to be exhaling. After a silence Will turns and looks at me.

•

Do you think you can do this? he says. I don't know what to say.

Well, I say, I don't know. I mean it's hard.

Really hard, he says, leaning back into the steps. School is hard enough without all this.

Quit, I say suddenly, like it's that easy. He finishes with the leaf and throws the bare stem down.

I can't quit, he says.

Why?

Because I just can't. The same reasons you don't quit.

I don't know why I don't quit.

Yes, you do. Everybody does. If you quit what's left? Studying? All you are is that guy who couldn't do it and everywhere you go that's what people are gonna think.

Not everybody.

I know not everybody but everywhere you go they're gonna be there. It's unavoidable. You can't go to a party without seeing them and besides, who wants to go to the parties that they're not at?

Lots of people.

That's bullshit and you know it, he says. People that don't matter go to those parties. These guys matter around here. He bends down and pulls his socks up around his pale ankles. I mean what would I be without this? he says. It's the first time girls have paid attention to me like they do, you know? I nod because I know exactly what he means. It's not like I've never had girlfriends before, he says, but with this it's different. I know it's shallow but I don't think I'd be much if I didn't go all the way through, and anyway pledging's only three months and after that you can do whatever you want.

You're right, I say and he is. Will stands up and brushes himself off.

I gotta go, he says. I look up and squint against the fading light.

Gotta study, he says, reaching out his hand. I clasp it firmly and it doesn't twitch. He walks down the steps and disappears around the side of Tillman. I bend down and take the bare stem that fell near my feet. Put it in my right pocket and for a long time I sit on the steps and let the orange light warm my face.

8

I OPEN THE DOOR to the Kappa Sigma hall quietly. Press in the silver bar gently and push forward. The outside air rushing in behind me. My pledge brother Kevin Brehm is leaning along the doorway of Dixon's jumbled room, arms crossed, skinny legs peeking through his frayed olive shorts. Dixon calls him a faggot. Says that he hates him. Kevin takes his words like gifts. Dixon tells him to get the fuck out of his doorway.

Bother someone else, he says when I pass by, his right hand swatting the air. I try not to look, walk with my head down but I can't help glancing up. Something in me wants to see what will happen but Dixon doesn't even look at me. I move quickly like I've avoided an accident and my heart is pounding against my rib cage and each step is in slow motion. I keep telling myself to just breathe and walk.

When I reach Brett's room I look back down toward Kevin and he waves, smiles a toothy grin, and I nod back but it's a short nod because I'm scared of the hall. I wonder how he's so at ease here. All smiles. He looks like a clothes hanger with his skinny neck and wide shoulders.

I can see Dave Reed hovering in the doorway of Ben Moore's room asking for an interview. A pledge has to interview all the brothers by the end of pledge season. The interview consists of simple questions: Who is your favorite band? What is your favorite color? Most brothers use this to get pledges to do something, like clean their rooms or fold their clothes. Dave's clutching his composition notebook tightly against his chest like he's holding a baby. Ben tells Dave that he's a faggot just like all his faggot pledge brothers but that he's especially a faggot because his hair makes him look like a bitch and he is laughing and yelling that Dave is a fucking faggot faggot faggot. The truth is that Dave is a faggot with hair like a girl because Ben Moore says it's so and we are pledges and there is nothing else.

IN HIS ROOM Brett plays the Refreshments on his stereo and it's good because it's minor chords and girls and drinking and being lonely and because sometimes it's good to be sad. Brett lights a cigarette, pulls on it hard, flicks red ash into a beer can and leans back into his burnt-red couch. Smoke fills the room. Filters into sunlight that streams through his grimy window, curls like thick fingers toward the ceiling. I reach for a tuft of smoke and it drips between my fingers.

Brett looks at me like I'm crazy then turns back toward the cracked wall. He stares a lot. At walls. People. Anything. Something will catch his eye and he'll just sit there with this look like it hurts and it's not just his eyes but everything, his clenched mouth and hands, his curved back. I lean against his wardrobe.

So, I say, looking around the room.

So what? he says. Smoke leaks from his mouth.

So how are you?

Me? I'm okay. He doesn't look okay but I don't tell him. He lays his left hand flat on one leg and with his other hand starts tracing the grooves between his knuckles. We just sit there and everything is quiet except for the music and the hum of his air conditioner.

I want to leave, he says, never looking up from his hands.

Leave? Leave where? I say.

Here. This place. I'm so bored with myself. With everything.

But you can't leave.

He looks at me for a moment and then turns back toward his knuckles.

I can, he says. Leans back and pulls from his cigarette, holds the smoke in his chest like he wants every bit. The look on his face scares me because I know that it's the truth. I know he can leave if he wants.

All right, motherfuckers, Dixon yells. I look around my brother's doorway and then back at Brett hoping he'll know what's about to happen but he keeps staring at the wall and blowing smoke.

Every one of you fuckers hiding needs to come out right now, he says. Dixon's voice bouncing off the walls. I step out into the hall and see Dave lingering in Ben Moore's doorway. I look at him like he needs to be out here with me but he just peeks around the corner and pulls back. Dave gets shoved out of the room, comes stumbling toward me. Drops his notebook and it makes a grinding sound skirting across the dirt in the hall. Dixon has Kevin by his skinny neck, one hand locked just below the ears, the other held straight up like he's about to say something important and Kevin is still smiling.

Line up, faggots, Dixon says. Ben Moore watches Dave bend to pick up his notebook. He knocks it from him again, and laughs, and this time it flies toward Dixon, who kicks it. The notebook opens in a flurry of white pages.

There are four of us. Me, Dave Reed, Will Fitch and Kevin Brehm and we all stand in the hall, clustered together, looking around and waiting for something bad to happen.

DIXON HAS A football. He says we're playing Goat Invaders, a game, he explains, created long ago which has survived because it's so much fun and this is how it goes:

We stand four feet apart, single file, all facing Dixon. We move our arms and legs in slow jumping jacks and bounce back and forth from wall to wall. It's supposed to look like Space Invaders. We bah like goats as we move and I don't know if the brothers are actually going to throw a football at us or if this is just meant to be scary. But what I do know is that Dixon says we better not fucking duck when he throws at us and that I feel stupid for moving like this waiting for a football to find me.

My feet grinding across the floor and I am second in line with Kevin at my front and Will and Dave at my back.

Don't you fucking flinch, Dixon says. He cocks one arm back and concentrates like it's the most important pass he's ever thrown. Ben Moore is behind us and he says come on,

Dixon, throw the fucking ball. Claps his hands together. I turn
my head slightly back toward Brett's room. He looks at me and
stands and then he shuts his door.

THE FIRST BALL skims Dave's head and bounces off the wall.

Oh, bad throw, Dixon says. Snaps his fingers. He claps his
hands, bends down and leans on his knees and says, all right,
Ben, let's see what you got.

I know the ball will hit the back of my head and I am waiting on it but Ben Moore has a good arm and he is not aiming
for me. Kevin winces when the ball hits the middle of his back.
The veins in his neck stand up. He keeps moving.

Sorry, goat, I was aiming for the bitch right in front of me, he
says, and he's lying but it works because I can hear Dave start
breathing harder behind me and he knows that it will hurt with
Ben only five feet behind him.

Kevin kicks Dixon the ball that's settled at his feet. Dixon
takes his time again and the ball makes a dull thump when it
hits Kevin's head. He doesn't pretend he's aiming somewhere
else, he just looks straight at Kevin and throws. Kevin stumbles
a bit, pauses and then goes limp. He drops down to his knees
and slumps against the wall. Dixon calls him a pussy and tells
us to keep moving and not to worry about our little bitch of a
pledge brother and we keep going back and forth until I hear
the ball smack something and the air behind me moves and I
know that Will's hit the ground. Ben Moore laughs behind us
and he's on top of Will telling him to get his sorry goat ass up,
get the fuck up, he says, what's wrong, your pussy hurt, huh,

your fucking pussy hurt? I keep moving and don't look back because I'm supposed to do what the brothers say.

Game over, Dixon says. He drops the football and walks back into his room. Dave and I stop moving and I look down at Will, and Ben is still standing over him, reaching beneath his armpits, trying to pull him up. He tries to stand but his legs wobble and he falls again. Ben slaps his head.

Pussy, he says and walks back into his room. Dixon leans back out because we are still standing around. He says to get the fuck off the hall. Will moves to his knees, lays his hands out in front of him and shakes his head like it's full of static. I grab his arm, help him up, but nobody helps Kevin. He's still sitting with his back turned, slumped against the wall. I open the door to leave and look back at Kevin. He's turned over, back flat against the wall, he's looking up at the ceiling and smiling.

OUTSIDE WILL IS still dazed and has to sit down on the front steps. I sit down beside him and Dave sits on his other side.

You okay? I say. Will puts his face in his hands. Right hand twitching.

Yeah, Will says, I'm okay, just a little dizzy. Dave shoves his hands through his hair. Stands up. I watch him walk across the quad and Will and I sit on the brick steps until his head is clear and he can walk without falling.

I START TALKING to myself. Walking to class, in the shower, in the cafeteria sometimes. I do it because there is no one else.

It is eleven on a Monday night and I am thinking about the pledge test we'll have in a few weeks and about Will and the way his hand shakes and the air is heavy and wet around the white concrete staircase that leads up to my dorm room. The football stadium at my back all lit like a holiday. I climb the stairs and start talking.

Why are you doing this? I say.

You know.

No, I don't know.

Yes, you fucking do, you know it's all there is.

I am more than that.

Wrong again, that's the wrong fucking answer, think, just think for a minute.

I pass a short dark-haired girl on the second flight and bite my bottom lip.

No, don't look at her, she can't help you.

It always happens like this. I can get to the point where I'm about to tell myself the answer, why I'm doing this, and then it just slips away.

I open the door to my room expecting to find my roommate plopped down on his futon smoking cigarettes. I close the door behind me and the room is filled with alcohol like someone's sweating bourbon. I put my books down on my bed and step on a hand. It crunches beneath my foot and I expect to hear a whine but when I turn around I'm still standing on the hand and the body connected to it doesn't move. One of my roommate's pledge brothers is lying on the futon all curled up like a baby. His right hand over the edge. Dark hair spilled over his eyes. I can't remember his name. He's snoring. I take my foot from his hand and sit down on my small bed. I stare at this boy who is drooling, all wrinkled and dressed in a coat and loosened tie and just then I decide that I hate him simply because he is alone inside his muffled head and I have to sit and listen to myself. I put my foot back on his hand and move it around, press it down into the floor to grind the bones but he doesn't move. I slap his head. He shifts a bit and then I go next door to get Mark.

Mark is from Kentucky and he's the biggest man I've ever seen. We talk in the bathroom when we shave sometimes, and I don't know why I am going to get him, but it just seems like the right thing to do. After I knock once he opens the door to his room and smiles. He has a forty-pound dumbbell in one hand, wears a blue tank top.

What's up, he says, one hand on the doorframe.

Nothing, I say, just that there's this drunk guy in my room and I've tried to get him up but he just keeps sleeping. I want you to scare him, I say.

Hold on, he says, turns into his room, places the dumbbell down at the head of his perfectly made bed. He leans down beside his bed and tells me to go on back to my room and just wait a second. I go and sit back down on my bed and stare at the boy who hasn't moved. Mark comes in with his shirt off, this long knife in one hand. He leans down close to the boy's ear. Mark is quiet like he's thinking really hard. And then he yells. It makes me flinch because I didn't know he could sound like this. I only thought he was big. But the boy stirs and Mark is yelling that he better get the fuck out of his room, that he is going to cut somebody. The boy's eyes peel open. He looks up at Mark. He doesn't know what's going on and for a second he just sits there and blinks at shirtless Mark clutching his knife and yelling for him to get his skinny ass the fuck out of his room. The boy rises and stumbles a bit, wipes his forehead and Mark is inches from his face, asking if he heard what the fuck he just said. His knuckles go white when he squeezes the knife. The boy looks at me and then at Mark. He is pale. Eyes blood-shot and then he is gone.

MARK AND I both laugh but mine is a sad laugh because I know the shadows I dream about, the smile and the breath, the brothers, they're filling me up. Mark clutches my hand as he leaves. I thank him.

Nothing to it, he says, I can't stand motherfuckers in my room either.

I WAKE UP when I hear the thump coming from downstairs. I stare at the clock and it says one-thirty and my eyes feel heavy even though I haven't really been asleep. I'm still dressed and I get up and walk to the door and press my ear against the cold metal. Gaze through the peephole and then I open the door and no one is on the third floor but the music is rising through the tiles under my feet. I can hear people moving. The brothers are having a party on the other side of the small dorm like they do on most Monday nights but I have chosen to stay away. It won't look good to the brothers but I have been shaking all day. I had almost fallen asleep but I'm always scared of my dreams or that someone will come pounding on my door at three A.M.

I LET THE door at the end of my floor fall behind me and walk the hallway that connects both sides of the dorm. I open the door on the Kappa Sigma side slowly and look down the hall. The third floor is quiet. I glance down the stairwell. Someone moves below me and I pull back and then I hear footsteps and no voices but someone is coming up and for some reason I just stand there. My heart pounding. A girl named Natalie drags her hands along the rail and wobbles a bit, turns her ankle sideways when she takes a step and falls down to her knees. She is still holding the chipped railing when she looks up. She reaches behind her and pulls each of her black high heels off. Her dress is black and short, cut low in the front and when she bends over her breasts spill out. She has both her shoes in one hand, straps wrapped around her middle finger and when she looks at me again I see her eyes for the first time. Swimming, teetering a bit as she blinks. She stands up and steps toward me.

Natalie is inches from my face and I can smell the alcohol on her hot breath. She sticks her tongue in my mouth and puts her hands around my hips. I pull away and look at her and we don't say anything. I take her hand and lead her down the hall toward my room and she drops her shoes on the way and doesn't look back.

Inside my room she takes my chin and pulls my face toward her and she smells like cigarettes and perfume and her mouth is slick and I don't even like her but, really, I love her for being here now. She moves in front of me, reaches around and clutches my back. The dim lamplight falling in bands across her stretched arms. The television painting her face. She slides against me. My hands on her hips, she takes my wrists and I let my fingers curl open slowly, she traces the grooves in my palms and pulls them to her breasts. My mouth is in her hair and my eyes are closed and she turns around and kisses me and I want to breathe in all of her, take every dancing cell into my mouth to keep from being alone. I crack my eyes to watch her mouth tremble, and everything is sleek from our open mouths and I close my eyes again. She pushes me down to the bed, hands against my chest and I feel like nothing and I want to tell her about all the dark things inside me, about the smile and the breath about the brothers and how they're fucking me up, but I don't, I just keep staring at her because I love her for kissing me and not saying a word. She touches my face with her hand. Lies down beside me. Closes her eyes. Her breath slow and warm against my face. I watch her breathe. When I wake up she's gone.

BRETT AND I leave on a Friday. Pledges are not supposed to leave on weekends but I do it anyway and Brett doesn't care. He drives and smokes and we pass idle cows and fields laid like grids and I keep expecting him to say something, to say anything, but he just stares and turns the radio loud. I roll down the window and let air rush through and I fall asleep with half of my head hanging out the window and for once my mind is quiet but I know that this peace is fleeting and that Monday will be silent and gray and we will have to come back.

OUR HOUSE SMELLING of damp and burnt wood. My parents beam, look at us like we've been gone for years. My mother looks at me and says I told you you'd be all right, and I want to say I'm not, I'm all wrong, but it wouldn't matter, she wouldn't understand, and even though she's a nurse, she couldn't help me at all. She's in bed by nine. My father, Brett and I stay up and watch television until my father is snoring on a recliner beside the fireplace in our den. Brett on the couch with a blanket pulled up over him. Me on a chair beside my father. I go over and stare down at him, put my fingers close to his face, flick his nose and he shakes, bleary-eyed, and Brett and I laugh and my father tells us to fuck off, rubs his eyes, waves a hand at us and goes down the hall to the bedroom. Deep snoring a minute later.

Man, Brett says, he can fucking snore.

Yeah, I say. No doubt.

You, too, Brett says.

Not like that, though.

You'll be there soon enough. In your blood.

Whatever. In the dark room the television punches light on Brett's face.

You remember, he says, how we'd come home late as shit and open the door all quiet and listen for those snores?

Yeah, I say. All the way from the back of the hall. Loud as a sonofabitch.

Brett laughs.

It's how we knew if we were cool coming home late, if we opened the door at two or three in the morning and could hear our father's snoring from the den. If we didn't hear it, we'd just sit outside and smoke cigarettes and then check again. My mother has trained herself to ignore the snoring but her ears were tuned to hear us, and if we weren't quiet enough, we'd wake her and she'd appear in the dark all drunk with sleep and ask us where we'd been and we'd say oh just watching a movie, started it late you know? She'd nod and stumble back down the hall. This is how my mother is. If she wakes in the night, she's delirious, doesn't know what's going on, but still stumbles around the house checking on us or cutting off lights we've left on, picking up shoes or books we've strewn around. My father, if he woke up for some reason, would just smell our breath and tell us not to be stupid and drive around drunk. We'd nod, say nah, man, we don't do that. He'd always say you know you can call me if you're drunk. I'll come get you.

BRETT AND I sit up and watch television for as long as we can and Matthew isn't home yet from his Friday night. My parents had had enough by the time he started high school, so he's pretty much free to do what he wants. Brett falls asleep and when I get up to go to bed, trying to be quiet, he looks up at me bleary and says night. It's always like that. I always try to get back to my room without waking him just to see if I can but he always wakes up. No matter how quiet I am. It's like he's asleep but part of him is always listening to see if I'm still there.

EVEN THOUGH I'M home I still dream the same fucked-up things, faceless men scratching at the windows of my room. I'd hoped it would help to sleep at home, that I wouldn't keep waking up in the middle of the night sweating and then lying still and waiting for the sun to come up. But it doesn't happen like that. It's the same thing. All the time.

SATURDAY AFTERNOON INSIDE a convenience store across from my house I'm buying cigarettes and the cashier tells me I'm going to die and I say what? and she says nothing.

I tell Brett about the woman when we're in his room Saturday night. He's in his bed reading something about Kierkegaard. I'm on the small couch against the wall. He turns a page.

Did you hear me? I say. He looks up from the book.

Yeah, he says. I heard you. Looks back down at the book.

Well?

Well what?

You don't think that's fucked up?

You probably misunderstood her.

No. I heard it. Plain as anything. She acted like she didn't say anything but I know she did.

I don't know, man. Even if she did say it, so what?

I just thought it was fucked up, you know? Telling me I was going to die.

We're all going to die.

Oh yeah that's fucking insightful.

I don't know what to tell you, man.

You think I'm crazy?

He looks up from the book. Closes it, holds a finger to mark the page and rests it on his chest.

No, I don't, he says. I think you misheard her or something.

I didn't, I say. I swear.

What do you want me to say?

I don't know. Just that it was weird.

It was weird.

You think I'm going to die soon or something?

No.

Why not?

I just don't. I mean I really don't know but I don't think so. Not like tomorrow or anything.

Okay. And then we're quiet. Me staring at the television that's turned down low. Brett at his book.

You sure? I say.

Yeah, he says. I'm sure. Don't listen to fucking crazy people like that.

Okay, I say. Then I drop it.

Brett looks up again from the book. Does this have something to do with the pledge thing? he says.

What? I say.

I don't know. Like stress or something.

Nah. I doubt it.

Brett stares at me. Just think about it, he says. Maybe it does.

Okay, I say.

I DON'T THINK about pledging and whether it stresses me because I know Brett's right. I leave the room and get into bed. I can't stop thinking about the woman and what she said and how I know I heard it. I fall asleep and wake in the middle of the night shaking again. Sit up straight in my bed. The television still on and muted. I turn it up and listen for the voices of reporters, salesmen, fitness instructors, whoever.

FIVE-THIRTY IN THE morning on a Monday and Brett and I leave to get back for class at nine and I sleep most of the way back and Brett just keeps smoking with the windows rolled up and listening to some sad crooner he likes. The glass cold against my face. The seatbelt draped under my chin to hold my head up. I keep nodding off and then the car shakes and wakes me up and my whole body quivers because I don't want to go back, I would rather just turn around or get out here or keep driving to anywhere and forget about everyone, forget about Will and Dave and all the brothers waiting on me.

But it doesn't go like that.

Brett pulls into the dorm, keeps the car running, we both just sit there.

Going to class? I say.

No, he says. Fuck class, I'm not going. Fuck this place. These people.

I don't say anything.

What are you doing? he says. You want to come with me?

Nah, I say. I need to go to class, and I'm lying, because I know he needs to be by himself and I know he can't help me right now anyway.

All right, he says.

I open the door and get out, reach back in for my bag.

Have fun, I say.

Yeah, he says.

I shut the door and he pulls out.

He doesn't look over his shoulder and then he's on the road, a car blaring its horn at him but he doesn't look back at it or at me. This is what Brett will do: drive on the interstate in any direction. It doesn't matter. Stare at yellow lines. Drive until he can't keep his eyes open. He's always done this when he can't think or is thinking too much. I am standing alone at nine o'clock with the quilted morning sky and the orange and yellow leaves raining around me like ashes.

I SHAKE ALL day.

On the way to class everything is livid. I don't know why. It just is. I can see the edges of things. I can barely walk and it hurts to look at things.

I keep my head down the whole way. Stare at cracks in the sidewalk.

IN RELIGION CLASS Whelan talks about the Tao. But I can't follow him because my head is somewhere else. I can't think. The smile and the breath, the brothers, these shadows everywhere.

When Whelan's up at the chalkboard writing something the girl in front of me turns around. Dark skin and brown hair.

Hey, she says.

Hey, I say. Look up at Whelan and he's still scribbling.

You're a Kappa Sig, right?

Pledge.

Yeah, that's what I meant. I'm Erin.

Brad.

Cool.

She smiles and turns back around and I take my fingers, plug

my ears until I see people bending beside their desks to get
books and leave.

ERIN STOPS ME in the hall. Touches my arm.

Hey, she says.

I look around, hope I don't see any brothers.

Hey, I say.

So, I'm pledging Kappa, she says.

Oh, yeah?

Yeah. It's great.

I don't know what to say to her because my mind is all over
the place. I scratch my head.

Okay, she says. So, maybe I'll see you around.

Yeah, I say. Maybe.

Bye.

Bye.

Erin opens the double doors.

AFTER CLASS IN my room I lock the door and turn the lights
off because the glare hurts my eyes. Everything hurts. The air
hurts, it hurts to breathe because I don't want to do this pledge
thing anymore because I'm scared of everything, of closing my
eyes, of waking at night but I'm also terrified of what I will be
without the fraternity, that I will be nothing, that I am already
nothing. I know it with each step and breath. I know it more
than any truth. I know I'm nothing.

AND THEN IT'S done.

I call my brother and when he picks up his phone I hear music blaring in the background. The Monday-night party that I'm supposed to go to.

Where are you? he says.

I can't come, I say. Can we talk for a second? He pauses, the phone scraping his chin. The music rises and he tells someone to stay the fuck out of his room.

Someone says excuse me, motherfucker. The door shuts and the sound shrinks. The air between us silent.

Where? he says after a moment and I can barely talk. I tell him I don't know where and he tells me in the stairwell that connects the two sides of our dorm, between the third floors, and I say yes, that's fine, and I know he hears the salt in my voice, my shaking hands.

BRETT SITTING ALONE on the top step. Waiting for me when I open the door. I walk to the stairwell slowly, and he tells me not to worry, there's no one around, but I worry anyway.

I smooth my jeans out, pull the hat down over my eyes. Brett takes a pull from his cigarette and thumps it against the wall. It bounces, sends red ash like sparks from hot steel. One branch from an oak bounces against the window in front of us. Brett takes a drink from his beer.

After the drink he says talk and I don't want to because I know I will cry. I can feel it coming already.

It's hard to talk, I say and he nods, stares at the glass, brings the beer to his lips again. I open my mouth again and I can't say anything. I drop my head against my chest. We sit and I cry and

Brett says nothing. The door opens to our right. I look up and my face is all wet and red and Chance stops when he sees us.

Whoa, he says and Dixon is behind him. He peeks over Chance's shoulder and I bring my head down again. Brett turns, springs up, rushes at them and grabs the doorframe. He slams it closed and pounds his fists against the green metal.

Stay the fuck out, he yells, stay the fuck out. He pounds his fist into the door again and backs away. Throws his beer against the door and foam spirals over the floor and he kicks the can against the wall.

Goddamn you, he says, I fucking hate you hate every one of you fucks. He backs away and lowers his head, brings a hand to his forehead. Sits beside me again.

I'll tell them you're done, he says.

I don't know, I say, maybe I should stick it out.

He shakes his head.

No, he says, you're done. I'll tell them tomorrow.

I want to tell him that he's all I've got left and I'm terrified of being alone, that maybe these brothers are all I've got, that I'm scared of them but I'm scared of what I'll be without them, but nothing comes out and I just sit there with my head bowed.

Brett gets up.

Lock your door tonight, he says, and don't answer if someone knocks.

He steps back down the stairwell and the door downstairs opens and thick music lifts and the oak taps the glass again softly and through the haze I can see the moon cut by dark leaves.

I PASS FROM them quietly, and then nothing's left. No one remembers my name.

Brett tells the brothers the next day that I am done and they act worried, concerned, and want to know if everything is okay with me. He tells them I'm fine and they all nod, hands laid flat over the pleats in their khakis. Eyes pinched into small slits. There is no ceremony to strike my name, no ritual to simulate my death, no walking the gauntlet between rows of brothers and pledges, each head falling like a domino, eyes turned down to the floor as I pass. This is how it goes:

Brett speaks.

They nod.

I vanish.

9

DON'T KNOW WHAT to do with myself after I leave the fraternity. I still feel their eyes on me everywhere but now it's different. It's fear and shame. I'm scared to see them, to see the look on my pledge brothers' faces that says you left you left us and the look on the brothers' faces that says pussy I knew you were a pussy I knew you couldn't do it. When I see them I duck my head, skirt my eyes toward a building or tree or anything but I can feel their eyes on my back all the time and they're laughing. The dreams still come every night. This thing inside me I can't get out.

And my fears are right. I have nothing without the fraternity. I don't lose Brett but I do lose him. Something is cut between us. Again. But I know it's how it's got to be. He's got to be away from me because I'm fucking him up. I stay on my side of the dorm and he stays on his and it's not some regulation it's just the way it goes.

WE TAKE A field trip for Geology class and the hippie teacher leads us out past campus into these thick woods. Down into a ravine. Clay rising on each side. But I can't keep up. I keep thinking about Brett and how he's fucked, about me and how I'm fucked, how I don't sleep and how my head won't ever be quiet. There's this kid named Doug who has long hair. The only one I can talk to. Not because he's really interesting. He just never asks about what I do. Who I am.

The hippie teacher points up toward the clay walls inside the ravine.

Notice the striations, he says.

We all nod.

We can see time here, he says.

We all nod.

On the way back I bend down and pick up a small rock. Granite. Put it in my pocket.

I HAVE THIS one friend named Matt who's a Phi Delt but he doesn't care anything about it. Lives a floor below me.

Matt's five-seven and full of muscle and we work out to kill the time even though he's got a busted ankle from intramural soccer. He never says a word about me quitting the fraternity. He doesn't make fun of me. He doesn't laugh or call me a pussy.

I come into Matt's room on a Wednesday night at eleven when my head won't be still because I'm scared of the dreams

I know I'll have. Matt sits on his yellow couch with his bad leg perched on a coffee table.

We watch *Rocky* and after the movie's over Matt's girlfriend Babs calls. He moves into the corner beside his desk to talk. He yells and tells her she's fucked up fucked up, what the fuck is your fucking problem, he says.

Then he hangs up.

Babs calls again and he says don't fucking call me again tonight I've had enough of your bullshit and then he slams the phone down, picks up his small coffee table and throws it against the door. It breaks in half and the beer cans and ash-trays go all over. He throws the door open and stomps out into the hall. I follow him and he's leaning against the wall.

I hit him as hard as I can in the stomach once, drop my hands, stare at him like it was the most natural thing to do. I don't tighten my stomach for his punch and he looks at me like I'm crazy. He smiles and hits me, my eyes water and he lets his hands drop to his sides just like I did. I hit him again and it goes over and over until I can't breathe and we fall down laughing and sobbing and clutching our guts. Matt gets up and puts his hand through the glass case of a fire extinguisher, just turns around without flinching. He has pieces of glass in his knuck-les. He pinches his fist open and shut, pulls out flakes of glass, the blood dripping on the floor and I'm still on the ground holding my stomach and he just laughs and I laugh because there's blood everywhere and there's nothing else to do but laugh after we've beaten each other breathless.

I do this because it makes me forget. Because the pain is real. Because it's in my gut and not behind my eyes.

WILL FORGETS ME. Dave forgets me. I know it. They all forget me and I can't forget them. I love them. I hate them. I am dead. I never existed.

TOILET. WILL'S HANDS in a toilet down on his knees kneading a banana. He thinks it's shit.

Squeeze it, they say.

Get it in those fingers.

Yeah.

Mash it up.

Uh huh.

How's that shit smell?

How's my shit smell?

You're shit boy.

Goat.

Fucking goat.

He's gagging. Eyes closed.

Don't open your eyes, boy.

Shit boy.

Fist on the back of his head. White behind his eyes.

You gonna eat that shit.

Swallow it.

Pulled away. Stumbling with the shit on his hands. Dropping from his fingertips. Water over his hands. Open mouth. Fingers pulling his jaw down.

Open wide, they say.

Will can feel his throat locking.

Don't worry, goat, they say. No more shit.

And it's on his tongue, his throat clenches, and he swallows. Again and his mouth burns.

You thirsty, boy?

Thirsty, huh?

Hot shit.

Will's face shoved down into a cooler. Water lapping the sides, he's swallowing again, pulling it all down.

Here is what's in the cooler:

Water. Phlegm. Pubic hair. Piss.

I know he's doing this. Brett tells me. He had to do it once too.

10

THREE WEEKS AFTER I quit Brett calls me. Out of the blue. We've talked a few times since everything went down. Sometimes I ask him what the pledges are doing. Mostly, though, it's nothing more than hi, Mom and Dad say hi. And I know it's not because he's mad or disappointed, it's just that he doesn't know what to do, and I don't either, so we leave it that way.

Brett wants me to come down to his room and I say I don't know, I don't want to see those guys and he says fuck them, they aren't around anyway. They're all at a mixer with Kappa, he says. I don't ask why he didn't go. I already know. He's pushing himself away from them. From everything. Because he can't stand himself anymore.

I LOOK THROUGH the window of the door to the Kappa Sigma hall. Brett's door is closed. My hands are shaking but

I push the door open anyway. Just don't look, I tell myself, don't look over and you won't have to see them. I'm afraid I'll see Ben Moore and he'll call me a pussy or just shake his head back and forth. I walk quietly and knock on Brett's door.

He says come in. His voice opaque through the thick metal door. I push it open and he's sitting staring at the television, the lights off, the volume down.

Hey, I say.

Hey, he says and I sit down in a metal chair and it's cold through my T-shirt.

I stare at the television and I know he's looking at me.

Do you want to leave? he says. I'm leaving.

Tonight? I say.

Yeah, tonight.

Where to?

Charleston, he says. To see Chrissie and to just leave. Chrissie's his sometime girlfriend.

I don't know, I say. Kind of late for that, you know?

Okay.

Okay? I didn't say I wouldn't.

You won't, he says, and he's right; even though I want to leave with him some part of me can't. Everything is quiet and then he stands up.

I'm going, he says. He looks over at me. At my pockets. What the fuck's in your pockets?

Nothing.

Getting big, man.

Drop it.

Okay.

Bye.

Bye, he says, and then I'm up. I know he's right about my pockets. I can't stop keeping things and I don't know why. I pull the door and when I turn around the television is off and the room is dark and Brett is standing in the corner staring out into the cold.

I GO OUT onto the side stairwell and look down into the parking lot. Brett's car pulled up on the grass. The wind blows, pulls the wet scent of garbage from the trash bin below me.

On the wall next to me in blue marker someone has written this:

Phi Delts suck cock.

Beneath that someone has written this:

Your mother sucks my cock.

I hear a door slam while I'm reading the wall and I look down and Brett's lights blink on. The car cranks and begins to back up and for a moment I want to run down and leave with him but I know it will just have to be like this for now.

My feet won't move.

I watch Brett's car grow smaller and then he disappears when the oaks swallow him.

WILL'S NEW NICKNAME is Ghost Fitch. It's because he's never around. His excuse is that he's busy with schoolwork. Architecture major. But the brothers don't care.

This is what they say:

School is the most important thing.

This is what they do:

Yell and scream and hate if you don't show your face.

Will's a ghost.

My brother tells me this on a Tuesday in mid-November.

NOW I CAN'T throw anything away. I've been saving things for a while but now it's everything. It all gets stored in my pockets or under my bed.

These are the things under my bed:

Letters from my mom and dad.

An article my grandfather sent me about a local high school student who has sworn off alcohol, tobacco, drugs and premarital sexual intercourse.

My pledge paraphernalia:

The *Bononia Docet,* which I haven't given back.

Invitations to pledge week functions.

An alphabetical list of my pledge brothers.

An alphabetical list of the brothers.

A photocopy of the Star and Crescent.

My bid from Kappa Sig.

A baseball bat.

A bloody T-shirt.

These are the things in my pockets:

Receipts. From cigarettes. From food. From anything.

A campus map.

My class schedule.

A leaf.

Movie stubs. *Trainspotting. Beautiful Girls. Heavy. Jerry Maguire. Swingers. Ransom. James and the Giant Peach.*

A watch that doesn't work.

A Band-Aid.

A key.

A tiger cut from an Exxon gas card.

Pennies.

A small glass bluebird.

Cigarette wrappers.

A green string.

Used books of matches.

A gold earring in the shape of a heart.

One medium-sized rock. Granite.

One clear blue plastic lighter.

They make my pockets bulge like I'm carrying small animals down there. I think I do it because these things are tangible, because I can hold them in my hands and because I know that if I don't something bad will happen. That the things I dream will find me. Brett doesn't say anything else about my pockets sticking out or the way I have to pull out wads of trash every time I look for my keys or my money. When I walk everything rattles and I have to shove my hands down deep to hold the pennies and the trash so the noise won't be too loud.

I READ ABOUT the girl and the dam on a Monday after I leave class. Mike's standing there beside the pile of student newspapers and I say hey man and he says hey man. Mike's a Phi Delt from Pittsburgh, all gruff with a beard he never shaves. I don't mind being around the Phi Delts because they never ask me about fraternities. They know I quit Kappa Sig and they don't care. Mike says so Thanksgiving huh you going home huh and I say yeah day after tomorrow or tomorrow I don't know. He nods, pulls out a smoke and lights it and then holds the pack toward me. I take one and light it. Fucking turkey Mike says and I say yeah fucking turkey. When he leaves I get a newspaper. I sit down on a bench and cross one leg. I'm reading the front page. At the bottom there's a small article about a recent student death. Emilia Bright from Connecticut and she was a sorority pledge. Found bobbing facedown at the base of the Lake Hartwell dam.

I tear the article out and cram it down into my jeans with everything else.

WHEN I KNOCK on Brett's door he's up in his bed with a hand hanging over the rail into the empty space between the floor and the loft. I pull on his index finger and he turns over, looks down at me.

What? he says.

I need your car.

What's wrong with yours?

In the pit. I saw yours outside.

Why?

I have to go somewhere.

Where?

The dam.

He sits up and rubs his cheeks.

Gonna jump?

No. Not yet.

Okay.

He drops down from the bed and pats his jeans, goes over to the windowsill and picks up his keys. I didn't expect him to come but when I look at him I know that we've made this turn back toward each other. That now we're going to be fucked together.

THE DAM IS whitewashed concrete all the way down to the lake. Brett touches my shoulder as I lean over and we stand on the edge with our toes sticking out over the concrete and I'm scared of heights but I want to see what the girl saw when she went over into the water. If she could feel the air rush into her face.

Brett stands there looking over the edge.

Let's both do it, he says.

Okay, I say. Lean forward again out over the edge. Look for the girl. Brett puts a hand on my shoulder.

No, he says. Not yet.

I stare at the water. It's still and the girl's there floating face-down the hair stretched out around her head like weeds. She dips over the rise of water. Arms and legs stretched like some star. And I don't know why I love her but I do. Brett touches my shoulder again and says careful and then the girl's gone. I squint my eyes to see if I can find her below the dirty brown water. Staring up at me. Smiling.

WE WATCH *The Natural* in Religion class. The girl in front of me with a Kappa shirt on. Big embroidered Greek letters across her chest. She's hunched and I can see her shoulder blades poke through her shirt. I can't stop staring at the shoulder blades, the way they make the fabric rise and fall. She turns around and looks at me like I'm bizarre, like I know something I shouldn't. I want to tell her that it's nothing, that I'm not strange and that I knew her once when I was a pledge and she smiled at me then told me her name was Erin and that just now I didn't mean anything by staring at her shoulder blades but she just turns around and hunches again.

I CROSS BENEATH a brick arch that leads from the quad to downtown, where I'm going to buy a compact disc of this band called the Descendents and after I do I keep the receipt.

After I leave the record store, I go back toward the quad, down Main Street, all the bodies pushing past me, the voices, this chatter and hum everywhere. I keep my head down, focus on the cracks in the sidewalk, start counting, make sure not to touch one with my feet, make sure that my right foot steps over a crack first because it makes perfect sense now to do these things and I'm looking down and I hear someone call my name. I look over and stop my feet and there's this girl named Tara Powers who I went to high school with and who I thought I might have loved once. She's at a stoplight with the passenger side window rolled down, leaning over across the seat, saying hey you hey you, waving her hands toward the car and then I forget about the cracks and I'm walking over to the edge of the sidewalk. Tara tells me to get in.

WE DRIVE. LEAVE downtown and take the road that leaves campus. She looks at me while she's driving.

So Eric, she says.

Who? I say.

Boyfriend. You know him. He's a KA.

Heard of him.

Well, he's a shit.

Oh yeah?

Shit, that's what he is.

Okay.

Not really.

Oh, I say. Listen. I turn around. Look behind me at the tops of dorms jutting out over the trees. Where are we going?

To my place.

Why?

Just because.

All right, I say and we drive to her apartment, which is in this complex with nothing but students.

Inside her apartment she drops her bag on a coffee table littered with magazines. Tara sits on the couch. Puts her face in her hands.

That fucker, she says. I know he's fucking that girl. There's a Van Gogh print on the wall. A *Pulp Fiction* poster. I'm standing by the door. She looks up at me. The brown hair. Pale skin.

You can sit down you know, she says.

All right, I say and then I sit down.

You want to watch TV? she says. I say yeah. She turns on the television, it's some cowboy thing with the horses and the guns and the red rocks everywhere.

This cool? she says. Turns her head to the wall.

Yeah, I say. She runs her hands through her hair. One of the cowboys gets shot off his horse and falls down.

Whoa, I say.

What? she says. Turns and looks at me.

That cowboy he just got shot and fell off his horse.

I look over at her and she's still looking at me. She takes my chin and pulls my face to her and her mouth opens, her tongue inside my mouth and my tongue on hers all wrapped and she kisses me hard and I kiss her hard back.

And then she pulls away from me. I sit back against the couch. Scratch my chin. On the television another cowboy drops.

Sorry, she says.

For what? I say.

For that. I shouldn't have done that.

Oh, that was all right, I say. Fine. Good. You kiss good.

We watch the cowboy movie and she reaches over and holds my hand.

And it's fine that it's been this way with girls for a while now, these random things, because I know I'm too much for anyone, that if I let myself, I'd love them all, I'd think they could fix me. But I know they can't, and it's enough, because every so often when a girl kisses me, touches my hand, my face, I remember that the world has light.

On the way back she keeps looking over at me and I don't

know what to say. She pulls up into the dorm parking lot. Keeps the car running. I open the door and step out. Look back into the car.

Bye, she says. Thanks for that.

I nod. Shut the door and watch her drive away.

11

THE DAY BEFORE THANKSGIVING.

The pledges have a week left.

I call Brett and no one answers. I'm supposed to ride home with him. When I go down to his room there's a note on the door. A piece of torn yellow paper with my brother's jagged writing. This is what it says:

Brad.
Fuck man had to leave.
Ride home with Will.
Brett.

I knock on the door and Brett's roommate Wes answers.

Brett left last night about four-thirty, he says. Went to Charleston. I nod.

Thank you, I say.

BACK IN MY room I call Will.

Yeah, he says, Brett asked me to give you a ride. It's on the way.

Thanks, I say.

It's cool, I'll be out front at six, he says. After my lab.

I don't want to ride with Will but he has to pass right through Florence to get home. I've gone the last few weeks without seeing him. Or Dave. I've only had to see brothers or pledges at a distance. When I walk to class. In the cafeteria. I don't want to sit for three hours and be reminded of what Will's about to finish and what I left behind. If I had stayed it would have almost been over.

But I didn't.

That's what I'm left with.

I LEAN OVER the railing in the outside stairwell and wait for Will's car to pull up. Someone has added a new line to the wall directly underneath the one about someone's mother sucking someone's cock.

This is what it says:

Fuck you all.

And I can't stand looking at the lines anymore. I want them gone. I go into my room and get a black permanent marker. Scribble out the lines about Phi Delts sucking cock, about someone's mother sucking cock and the last line that says fuck you all. I cover each letter with the black ink and add my own line. I write my name.

I'M IN THE backseat of Will's car. He turns around.

Ready? he says. All smiles. The car a new-model gold Toyota Camry. Immaculate on the inside. A girl in the passenger seat. She twists around.

Anne, she says.

Oh hi, I say, I'm Brad.

Will puts the car in drive, stops and spins his head.

Oh man, he says, that was rude, Brad Anne, Anne Brad. Nods his head at us each time he says a name. Anne is wearing a heavy green coat, her long hair tucked beneath the collar. Her face is small and round and her hands are warm.

You like the Dead? she says.

Sure, I say, I like the Dead.

Even though I don't. It feels like the right time to lie.

Man, Anne says, I love Jerry, and we listen to a live show. I keep thinking of a bumper sticker the punk rocker who lives next door to me in Daniel has. It's on his door. It says Jerry's Dead. Shave Your Head. Anne turns around.

This is one of the best, she says. Fillmore '71. I nod and place my face against the cold window glass and for a moment I forget that I don't like the Dead and the cheers and music begin to blend with the quiet hum of the engine and Clemson slips behind us and we don't even notice.

I OPEN MY eyes when I feel the car stop. Will pumps gas and Anne smokes through a cracked window. She rests the cigarette against the slit and when she flicks her thumb against the filter the wind carries ash onto the windshield. It rolls down and rests against the wipers.

Will hunched over the gas nozzle, one hand shoved into his pocket. He keeps pulling it out, changing hands to pump. Shaking with the cold. Anne leans back and lets smoke dance beneath the overhead light. She smiles, takes two quick drags and stubs the cigarette out in the middle console's ashtray.

Still glad that you quit? she says. She knows.

Well, yeah, I say.

Really though I'm lying. I don't know if I'm glad. Not now. Not with everyone else so close.

Just wasn't for me, I say. Not my gig.

Yeah, she says, I know what you mean.

Did you? I say.

Did I what?

You know, pledge?

Oh, yeah. Chi-O. Not really a big deal though. I don't really care much about it.

I nod. The brothers taught us a song about Chi-O's. It goes like this: *Chi-ho Chi-ho it's off to bed we go with a Lambda Chi between my thighs and an SAE on top of me Chi-ho Chi-ho.* These verses then repeated.

We don't have to do crazy shit like you guys do, she says. I mean I understand why someone wouldn't want to do all that. Will's told me some.

Not much fun, I say. I turn back toward the window. Will running from the gas station. He opens the car door and plops down into the seat, rubs his hands together.

My God, he says, it's so cold. His hand twitches when he goes for the ignition. He cranks the car and turns the heat high.

ANNE HAS HER feet pulled up close to her chest. Arms
wrapped around her knees, head leaned against the window.
The seatbelt looped under her chin. No one's said anything for
about an hour. The Dead are still playing but it's a different
show. I think. It all sounds the same.

I lean up between the seats.

You must be excited, I say.

Oh, yeah, Will says, I am. It's almost over. One more week.

Cool. Been hard I know.

Yeah, really. I didn't know if I could do it.

You did, though. That's more than I can say.

He shakes his head.

You don't feel bad about all that, do you? he says.

Sometimes, I say. Yeah. A lot really.

Well, don't. You shouldn't. I mean it's easy for me to say that
now when I'm almost done. But really. You don't have anything to be ashamed of.

I just feel bad sometimes. Lonely, you know.

Yeah, I know. He reaches over into Anne's lap and takes her
cigarettes. He shakes the pack, brings a filter to his mouth.

Since when do you smoke? I say.

Since I became a pledge, he says. Want one?

Sure, I say. Take the filter he's shaken over the edge of the
pack. He cracks our windows and the cold air rushes through.
Stiff against my face.

I'm worried, though, he says. I squint my eyes against the air
blowing back.

About what? I say.

The vote.

The final one?

Yeah.

Why?

I haven't been around as much as they want. They call me Ghost Fitch.

Oh, I say like I don't know already. I wouldn't worry. I don't think they'd vote anyone out who made it this far. It's just a scare tactic more than anything.

Yeah, you're right, he says. I just worry about stuff. I'm a worrier.

Me, too. That's why I couldn't hack it.

I just got lucky I guess. I really don't know how I did it if you want to know the truth. You don't know how many times I almost quit. I just tried to stay busy with schoolwork.

Well, congratulations, though. You've done something that's really hard.

Thanks man, he says and I can feel the fear leave his voice. It's like someone has exhaled deeply, pushed everything out.

That means a lot, he says. From you. Really. It does.

Why?

Just does. All that shit me and you did at the beginning. I mean I still feel like it should've been me and not you sometimes. You know, who quit. You've got more guts than me.

I don't.

I think you do. You just don't know it. But anyway, thanks for the congratulations.

You're welcome, I say.

He shoots his cigarette through the crack in the window and exhales a stream over the edge. I flick my cigarette out and look back. Orange sparks over the concrete behind us. I turn back and catch Will's face in the rearview. His eyes are dancing and his hands lie silent on the steering wheel.

A GOAT CHAINED to a basketball post. Head bent, picking at the grass in the raised section of courtyard. Outline of jawbone poking back into his neck. My eyes are hazy because it's seven-thirty on the first day of exams. I rub them hard and blink to make sure the goat's really there. When I take a step down from Daniel Hall the goat looks up at me. Ribs poke through its wiry gray coat like curved fingers and small horns have come through the top of the skull. Breath billows from flared nostrils. The goat gives me a blank stare and then bends back down to gnaw at the dead grass. I lower myself onto the last step and watch through the cold. I'm shivering but the cold feels good and I start to rock back and forth, wrap my arms across my chest and begin to laugh. It begins as a slight heave but then I'm shaking with the cold and the laugh for this scrawny bristly chinned goat and for whoever left him here.

AT MY GEOLOGY exam everyone looks drugged or dead. The girl next to me taps her pen and digs at the corners of her eyes, looks at each index finger and wipes them on her torn jeans. The baseball player still has his arm in a sling and has to write with his left hand. I am staring at the blackboard, at the coiled chalk smudges and I haven't even looked at my exam. The hippie teacher walks through aisles and looks over our shoulders. When he passes by I feel his eyes on me telling me I better get to work but my hands won't move because I don't care. His patchouli makes me wince. When I pick up the pencil I mark C for every question.

In three days Will and Dave will be brothers.

In three days I will be gone and I won't come back.

I get up and leave my test on the desk and the hippie teacher doesn't even look up. It's December and he's wearing a heavy pullover and shorts, leaning on the big desk up front, playing with this geode he bobbles like a grapefruit.

THE KAPPA SIGMA hall is silent. It smells like a cow pasture and I scrunch my nose. I try the knob on Brett's door and it slides open. The room is dark. Brett's arm is dangling from his side of the loft, head turned toward the wall. I touch his palm and trace the lines of his hand with my thumb. It twitches when I get to the soft part near the lifeline. I grab his wrist and pull, his eyes tear open, he inhales like it's his first breath.

What? he says. What are you doing here this early?

I thought you had an exam, I say. This morning.

What?

An exam. A final. This morning.

He looks around like he doesn't know where he is.

What time is it? he says. Rubs circles across his eyes.

It's like nine, I say. Maybe ten after.

He falls back into his pillow, rubs his eyes again and lets out a slow oh fuck.

Fuck fuck fuck, he says.

What time was it? I say. He rolls over, places an open palm against the wall.

Eight, he says. Fucking eight o'clock. I laugh.

It's not funny, he says.

Yeah, I say. You're right. And then I laugh again.

Fuck it, he says. Whatever. He pulls the sheets back over his bare back.

I close his door softly behind me and the pasture smell hits me again. I look down and there are hoofprints in the floor dirt.

BRETT TELLS ME this after he wakes up at one:

Last night the pledge class steals a goat. Twelve of the pledges drive in two separate cars to a farm forty minutes outside Clemson. Two pledges jump the barbed-wire fence at two in the morning, step in shit, lead the goat through a gate and lift him into the back of one pledge's red extended-cab Chevrolet truck. The goat doesn't put up a fight and sits still the whole way back. Like a baby. Somewhere around four they open the doors to the Kappa Sigma hall, lead the goat by a dog leash they'd bought at Wal-Mart, go into the bathroom on the first floor and tie the goat to a stall door handle. A pledge feeds the goat some dog food. Also purchased at Wal-Mart. Puts four tablets of Extra-Strength Ex-Lax into the food because he figures the goat is big but he's really not and after all animals probably need more to induce diarrhea because their stomachs are strong and a goat has the strongest stomach of all. They eat aluminum cans. One pledge shuts off the lights in the bathroom when they sneak out but another wants to leave them on because he doesn't want the goat to get scared so they leave the lights on and let the door fall shut.

I HAVE ONE more exam and then I'm gone. It's four-thirty on a Thursday and everything is slow. Have my window open because the day has been mild. The only sounds I hear are an occasional car whirring by. I try to study but the test is on British Literature like Milton and Keats and I don't care about those guys much right now. My teacher is old and boring and doesn't really want to teach. Has never looked at us the whole semester. Always stares at the back wall. Talks over our heads.

BRETT'S HEAD IN his hands when I open his door. Turns one eye toward me from beneath the hands and it is bloodshot. The whole hall quiet. All the doors closed. I expect everyone to be running around like mad because pledge season ended last night after the final vote. But it's not like that. The room dark. Spread hanging down from the foot of Brett's bed. I ask what's wrong.

You don't know, he says.

Nah, I say, what's going on?

Will, man, he says. He's dead. A heart attack. You don't have heart attacks when you're eighteen. Just fucking dead in his room. Like that.

I can't think straight.

This place, he says. Pulls hands back through his hair. This fucking place. He slides his hands down across his face.

I sit down on the couch beside him and lean back.

So they voted him out, you know, he says.

What do you mean?

Last night at the final vote.

I didn't think they could do that.

I've never heard of it.

I thought the vote was just a formality.

It usually is. But they can still do it.

I feel like I should be screaming or running through the halls and opening doors and pulling people out, throwing them like dolls, beating them with my fists. But I don't feel that. I don't feel anything except this high-pitched whine in my left ear.

Who was it? I say. Were you there?

Yeah, he says. I had to be.

You didn't have to be anywhere.

He looks at me like I'm crazy.

You don't know, he says.

You're right, I say. I don't.

They wouldn't listen. Fucking Chance and Dixon and Ben. You have to have two. Will had three.

When did they tell him?

Last night. After the vote. Late.

Brett lights a cigarette. Hands it to me and I take it and he lights another one and puts it between his lips. Takes a long drag and blows it out.

And today, he says, he just comes in his room after he's been studying, starts talking to his roommate. That Chris Sample kid. Then he's dead. Just like that.

It wasn't anything to do with the vote?

You don't die from a vote.

Still.

I get it, man, but you know we can't know shit like that.

I don't care. Those fucks did this to him.

I get up to leave and Brett grabs my hand, holds it for a moment and then lets go. I put my hand on top of his head.

You wanna kill them? I say.

Yeah, he says. Let's. Tomorrow.

When I walk outside the air smells like burning leaves. I look around the courtyard and the goat is gone and there's nothing to look at besides the clock tower at Tillman. I wait for a chime but the bell holds silent.

MY LAST EXAM is in British Lit and I don't care about my grade at all. Because I'm done. I'm gone. For the essay question I write my name. That's all I write. Brad. And I can't match any of the passages to authors on the other part of the test. My pen moves and the words mean nothing and I'll fail and I'll leave today and bury Will tomorrow.

I LOAD EVERYTHING into my car in the rain. Drop the key off in the housing office and come back to the dorm.

I want to walk through one more time before I leave and I want there to be a shrine. I want to see weeping. I want incense and priests and altar boys crossing themselves. Contrite hearts. A procession. Dixon carrying a cross on his back. Pictures of Will everywhere. I want a posthumous induction with all the sacred rites and I want to see it on the news. I want interviews and brothers sobbing about what a loss it was and how they plan to honor his memory in some grand and significant way. A scholarship. A statue. A memorial. But the hall is silent.

I knock on Brett's door and no one answers. Knock again and look behind me when I hear a door open. Chance McInnis takes one step out into the hall and looks at me. Takes off his white baseball cap and scratches under his chin. Coal black hair mashed down around his forehead. Barefoot. He stares at a spot on the floor. Spits. Turns around slowly, steps back into his room and closes the door.

I DRIVE HOME in the rain and when I get there I go to my room and shut the door and sleep.

This is what I dream:

There's Will all balled up on the ground. Holding his legs up against his chest. And we're all there. Me. Brett. Chance. Everybody. We're all standing around him in this circle. Brett kicks him first. Then Chance. Then me. But Will doesn't move. The feet just keep landing on him and he doesn't whimper or scream or flinch. And there's no end to it. This kicking. It keeps on. And Will's eyes are always open. Not looking up or at us. Just open. Staring out in front of him. Across the floor. At the feet when they split his jaw.

MY FATHER SHAKES me awake the next day.

Hey, he says. I rub my eyes, look around and for a minute I don't know where I am. The fan above my head whirs, makes the room move. The pages of a book next to my bed flap with the air. He touches my forehead.

Hi, I say. What time is it?

You gotta go, he says and then he turns and pulls the door shut softly behind him.

From the hall I see my mother sitting on the couch, legs pulled up against her chest and coffee in one hand. She's staring at something and when I touch the door to my brother's room, she turns her head to the hall, stands up and walks toward me. She's still holding the coffee, and I have my hand on the doorknob, she looks at me like she's studying my face.

I'm sorry about what happened, she says. Sorry about all of it.

It's all right, I say. It's okay.

She goes back to her room and shuts the door.

I open the door to my brother's room and he's bunched up on one side. I almost step on Chance McInnis's head. He's asleep on the floor. He had to spend the night because our town is only an hour from the funeral and his is farther away. I shake the doorknob so Brett will wake up. He pulls his eyes open slowly and closes them when he sees me standing beside his bed.

We're gonna be late, I say.

Okay, he says without moving. Okay. Chance shifts below me and when I look down at him I want nothing more than to judge him, to ask what he is doing on my floor, to make him leave, push him out into the cold morning air with nothing and watch him shake and shake and shake.

12

INSIDE THE LUTHERAN CHURCH people packed tight, mashed together into long polished wooden pews. Four stiff older men handing out programs and shaking hands. The stale air inside the church and the light from the stained glass in colored bands across the heads and shoulders of people seated in the pews. Brett and I pause a moment inside the vestibule, look down at our bulletins like there will be something taking place we need to know. But there isn't. It's a funeral and we're buying time before we make the long walk down the aisle across the gray carpet and nod toward people we know and grasp hands and rub shoulders. I let Brett take the first step and keep my head down because I don't want to see everyone heaving and the girls' mascara-streaked faces. I watch my brother's feet and we don't stop until we near the front. Brett stands back and lets me go first because he knows I don't like sitting on the aisle. He guards me. I haven't let my eyes move toward the front since we stepped inside the church but I can't keep them down anymore. I pray silently that the coffin will be closed and right now I don't even believe in God but I keep mumbling and raise my head and the coffin is closed. Its white planes gleam underneath the lights. Flowers placed carefully on both sides and on the closed lid and there's this picture of Will beside the coffin. He's smiling and I think it must be his high school senior picture because he's got on a tuxedo. His hair billows on the sides and I'd almost forgotten his face even though he's only been dead for a few days. I want to cry but nothing comes. The organist plays some soft hymn over and over, touching the keys and glancing up at her music sheet. I put my head back down and weave my fingers together in front of me. Someone's scratched the name Ritchie into the pew. The marks are childish and I like that they're here in all this perfect polished wood.

TARA POWERS COMES from the other side and sits down next to me. I look over when she nudges my shoulder and I don't know what to say. I hate all these required pats without words. But there are no words. She looks up front and then I feel like I should say something. I look up at her face and her makeup is streaked and she looks beautiful and sad with the light gleaming off her hair. I think about how she kissed me and how she held my hand and I'm trying to think of something to say like it's okay it's okay I know I know but everything seems wrong. The small light hairs running the length of her arm catch all the light. She pulls her hand up to her face. Shields her eyes. Reaches into her purse and pulls out a tissue, wipes the corners of her eyes and lets her hand fall into the space between us. She's still holding the tissue and I reach over and lay my hand across hers and she turns the hand up, puts her fingers between mine and the tissue is misty between our palms and we just sit motionless and clasp our hands tightly as the bodies fill in around us.

WILL'S FAMILY FILES down the aisle toward the family section. A brother who looks like a smaller version of Will leaning into his mother, she wraps one arm around his shoulder, tilts her head into his. Their eyes cloudy and filled with rain and no no no it shouldn't be like this they shouldn't have to weep for Will and goddamn this place goddamn all of this.

I look over at Brett and then he's in the coffin, his cheeks sunken and rouged, hands crossed over his waist and I'm in the family section and I tell myself it will never happen like this it will never be like this.

I SQUINT MY eyes hard and Brett's looking at me looking at him and he knows it too he knows it won't come to this. We will grow old and gnarled together and watch everyone die. He lays his hand on my knee and I put mine on top of his and we just sit there with the organ chanting thick notes and the light from outside settling on our heads and I can feel the blood throbbing through us both. I can see the cells moving through the raised veins in our hands and arms, I can see the hair growing on my brother's head, I can see his heart pulse and breathe and I know then that Brett and I will live forever.

We've seen too much. We know how the world tears people

open. But we hold the thought between us for a moment, let it live and breathe because it makes us like we were before, kids who knew the world could not exist without them.

THE PREACHER COMES from a side door and reaches the pulpit with ragged steps. He smooths the sides of his black robes and pushes his glasses up. His eyebrows twitch like they're snagged by fishhooks. He looks out over the patchwork of bowed and somber heads. The Bible in front of him open, he lowers his eyes, scrolls his index finger down the page. Brett shifts next to me, crosses one leg over the other. A bead of sweat runs down his forehead and his hairline looks damp. He swipes at it, lays his elbow on the pew's railing. I look back down at the etched name, rub my thumb over the grooves like I might gather some secret from its curves. Everyone stands and I shuffle with a hymnal and look over at Tara for the page. I don't sing and we sit down. The preacher starts talking about how it's hard to face a death so young and then he reads from the big Bible about Jesus being raised from the dead and Will was a good young man yes a fine young man and there's nothing to do but take comfort in the fact that Will is with Jesus now yes Will is with the Father with the Son and there's no pain and it doesn't hurt there it doesn't hurt anymore. I rub my eyes and turn my head. Look behind Tara. Pick out some brothers. Chance a few pews back. Ben Moore sitting beside him. And I look behind Brett to find more because they should all be here. Everyone. Our heads drop, and the preacher starts a prayer but I keep my eyes cracked, shift them to each side to make sure everyone is bowed. And I want to run to the front, take the microphone, stand in front of everyone and pound my fists on the pulpit, point out the brothers who got rid of Will, tell everyone, make everyone listen to me, these are the soiled, these are the impure, these are the men who choked this dead boy's heart. Everyone rises silently and outside the air is bright. The sharp wind bruises our cheeks. Brett walking beside me tall with the dress shoes and the sport coat and I keep stumbling over cracks in the concrete on the way to the car.

INSIDE THE TWELVE-YEAR-OLD black BMW my father has loaned us Brett and I smoke and listen to the radio. It's an oldies station with Sam Cooke singing some tune about never being good at Geometry or Biology but if you'd love him too what a wonderful world it would be. The air outside flows through the crack in the window and brushes Brett's hair back. He raises his cigarette to the slit, grazes the edge of the railing when he pulls it back in. Rubs the spot with his index finger and says fuck.

Doesn't really matter does it? he says.

What? I say and I think he's talking about life or death.

Burning this. He points to the mark he's left.

No. I guess not. We're smoking in here, right? I hold my cigarette up inside the car and it begins to gather in a thick cloud.

He won't notice, he says.

Dad?

Yeah. He knows anyway.

He's got an idea.

Yeah.

I raise my cigarette to the railing and burn a spot. Brett looks over with the smoke coming from his mouth.

WHAT I THINK will be a cemetery turns out to be a memorial garden. I'm used to weathered and crumbling granite and here the absence of headstones seems strange. A long row of cars pulls in ahead of us with blazing headlights. At the entrance a large American flag hangs limp. A thick white cross made of stone is planted in the center of a roundabout and we follow the line of cars toward the back of the garden.

Brett parks the car behind Chance's Blazer and we sit for a moment watching the cars pull in around us. Brett studies the rearview and then looks at me.

Hard, he says.

Yeah.

Look at all these people. He leans his head toward the crowd that is gathering around an open white tent.

What?

I don't know. Doesn't seem right. I nod my head. It's like everyone's all heaving, he says, but three days ago nobody gave a shit about Will. He wasn't anybody.

I liked him.

Brett looks at me and shakes his head.

Whatever, he says.

I did.

Yeah, and he was my best fucking pal, too.

I didn't say that.

You didn't even like him, though. I mean he was a nice guy. You're wrong. You don't even know.

THE DOORS ON the hearse open and a few men pull Will from the back. They drop the wheels and clasp the gold handles on the sides. Will's roommate Chris at one corner and they all walk with lowered heads toward the tent. Put Will in the middle of the tent where he's surrounded by standing flower arrangements. I notice for the first time that there's this arrangement of orange and white flowers shaped like a tiger paw and I think how insignificant it is. A school's colors and symbol. Behind and above the tent a large billboard that says the best shopping on the Grand Strand one mile ahead.

Okay, Brett says. Turns to me again. You liked him. So what. What does that matter?

It matters something.

Not really. You see that over there. Brett points toward the tent. That's him. In that box. They're gonna be throwing dirt on his face in a minute. And all these people are gonna think then, right then, that they loved him, they loved him so so much. He was everybody's best fucking friend. He shakes his head. He was nobody's friend, he says.

I don't say anything because I know he's right.

But you know, I say. Does it really matter? If we all love him for a second can't that be enough? The words feel flat in my mouth.

No, he says. That's not enough.

Chance gets out of his truck ahead of us and looks back. He nods and places his hands in his pockets.

Yeah, like that fucker, Brett says. You think that's love when Chance feels sad? Fuck no. That's not love. It's fucking guilt. All it is.

You're right, I say. I hate them too. I hate them for everything. I lean my head against the window.

Brett props an arm against his knee and rests his fist beneath his chin.

Well, he says. Looks over at me.

Yeah, I say and we open the doors.

I TRY NOT to step on any graves because I know I'm walking on dead people and I can see them snarling in their holes, baring their teeth like dogs.

Tara is standing a few people back from the front. She sobs, brings a hand to her face and the mascara rolls down her cheeks all black. She turns and sees me coming and holds her hand out. I take it between mine and I'm standing and holding hands with this girl that I barely know anymore and she squeezes her fingers tight like she loves me, like she won't ever let go. I keep my head down and people brush against my arms and then I'm closed in by all these black coats and over the tops of heads I can see all these brothers. Chance with his head bowed, his hands crossed in front of him. Ben Moore pats another brother on the back, shakes his hand at the same time like some official greeter, like he's giving a sales pitch.

All the whispers stop when the preacher moves under the tent. He reminds us again that Will is okay now that he's with Jesus. The pallbearers move the casket over a hole surrounded by green turf. Will's mother moves forward, puts a white lily on top of the casket and sobs into her hands. Her husband gathers her up and pulls her into his chest. Will's younger brother can't look at the coffin as it drops, he stands against his father like he will fall. Tara presses into me, wraps her arms around my waist. I look over at Brett and he's watching the coffin drop like he can see inside it and then he nods at Will when the coffin is slipping beneath the soil and I feel everyone around me, their breath, the pulse and sway of others.

ON THE HIGHWAY going home we don't talk, we just listen to the tires spin. The sun has settled into a deep orange, thin clouds strewn along its edges. I look over at Brett. He's got a wrist laid over the steering wheel, one hand settled in his lap.

The road stretches before us like some path we've never seen and the pines along the edge of the highway glow in the sunlight silhouetted at their backs. We open the windows all the way and the air is soft. I reach over and place my hand at the bottom of Brett's neck and squeeze. I leave it there and he reaches over, places his hand on my shoulder. We don't speak but we both know we won't go back to Clemson, that we won't ever go back, and nothing else is important, nothing more important than our hands and the air slipping inside to brush our faces. I let go of my brother's neck and his hand leaves my shoulder. He leans his head from the window. Drives with his eyes closed.

A NEWSPAPER CLIP my father gives me on Will Fitch the day after the funeral says these things:

Died suddenly after collapsing in his room on campus. Walked into his room and started talking to his roommate. Fell to the floor. The roommate called the Clemson University EMS, who transported him to Oconee Memorial Hospital, where he was pronounced dead at three thirty-three P.M.

AND LATER, IN my head, I watch Will Fitch fall down.

He opens his door and sees his roommate, Chris, at his desk, bent over a textbook. He takes a plastic pen from his shirt pocket, bites it with his back molars. He chews once and the heat begins just below his heart, the third rib, warms the bone and spreads in a dull wave. It's like ripples on a pond, opaque heat moving from the center and then his heart speeds and the hairs on his forearm and neck stand like soldiers. He rubs his ribs with a flat palm, kneads his fingers just below his heart and his legs give and he drops to the floor, sits staring at his roommate and his textbook and then Will's neck clenches and he is clawing at the mattress bringing knees one by one toward his chest like he's climbing but the light from the third-story window is blinding and white and spit bubbles at his mouth and he's shaking Chris stuttering no man what the fuck what the fuck oh God oh shit don't motherfucker don't don't don't motherfucker and the door opens and the air is sucked out of the room and he thinks so this is what it's like and how he expected something much more Lutheran something much more brilliant not just the spit and the heat and the ribs and Chris shaking his head like an idiot not just this oh God not just this but then he concentrates on the ceiling and the patterns pull him up and he is limp and his eyes are still and he sees nothing but this convergence of pattern and light and dancing flakes of dust and everything is at once still but also moving with a clarity he's never known and his chest and hair and heart and tongue are silent as if in prayer and then it is black and then it is nothing.

THREE DAYS AFTER Christmas I drive back to the memorial garden. Because I want to see this place alone. In the quiet.

The memorial garden like a grid. I turn in, follow the road to where I know Will is. Park my car and get out and it's cold and bright. The flowers marking the graves like hands, these plaques with the names everywhere and I'm walking where I think he is but I don't see his name, it's nowhere.

IN THE OFFICE at the back, I stare at the different plaque designs on one wall. This skinny man with glasses clears his throat, he's beside me.

May I help you? he says.

Yes, I say, I'm looking for someone.

Who?

My friend he's buried here. I can't find him.

The man nods. When was he buried?

Like a week ago, I say and he goes to a back office, comes out with a ledger, stands in front of me thumbing through it.

Last name? he says.

Fitch, I say.

First name?

Will.

Oh, Fitch, yeah. He turns the pages, runs a finger down and stops.

You couldn't find him because he doesn't have a marker. I nod but I don't understand. He holds the ledger in front of me.

See here, he says, this is where he is and he's pointing at this map with all the last names. So what you want to do, he says, is find Cantey comma Robert, take two steps to the left and you'll be standing on top of him. On Fitch comma Will.

I want to ask why there's no marker but I don't. I thank him and go outside.

I FIND CANTEY comma Robert. Take two steps to the left. Nothing but dirt. A billboard in front of me says Jesus is coming. A leaf falls at my feet. I bend down to pick it up and it's plastic, fallen from someone's fake flowers, and I think it's supposed to mean something but I can't figure out what and I'm staring at the ground and I can hear Will talking, his voice rises, spreads in waves around me and I feel it hoist my arms and I open my mouth to breathe it all in and I am shaking, and I listen to my dead friend, my feet on his ribs, roots from a nearby oak woven through him like careful threads and he says that I must remember him, I must remember how this place, this soil, these roots hold him like this late-December day holds the dizzy light and dense air.

I put the leaf in my pocket, and at home, that night, I dream this: Will on the floor of the hall. Balled up. And we're all there again: me, Brett, Chance, everybody. We kick him, but then he stands, and Brett's still there but everyone else is gone, and we're outside in the quad, we're all huddled together, breathing the speckled light, spinning, eyes drunk with the day and the light, with all this, with this braided brilliant dance.

BRETT AND I go to the road where my thing happened almost a year and a half ago. It's his idea. Because it's his thing too. Even though we've never said it, we both know it.

It's two days after New Year's. Takes us a long time to find it and I don't really know how we do but when we do we stop the car at the head of the road and sit there for a long time just staring. My heart is pounding and my hands are sweating.

So, Brett says. You ready?

I nod.

Yeah, I say.

I'm glad to finally see this place, he says. He squints his eyes. Looks down the road.

I'm glad you're here, I say.

I wanted to be. You know that. He's still squinting.

We open the car doors and step out and beneath my feet I can feel the same sharp granite. I bend to touch it, take one rock in my hand. Black and gray with the sharp faces that catch the sun. I look over at Brett. He's bent down touching the rocks with a flat hand. Picks one up. Turns it over in one hand. Looks up at me.

I've been here before, he says. Still holding the stone. Stands up. I look over at him.

Not really, he says. But it feels like it. I could see it all along. He puts the rock in his pocket.

I turn from him and look down the road. Reach inside my pockets and pull out all the receipts the campus map the class schedule all the movie stubs the stone the matchbooks the green string the small glass bluebird the used lighters the plastic tiger cut from an Exxon gas card the Band-Aid all the change and crumpled cigarette packs the plastic leaf I got from Will's grave. I hold them there in two hands and they spill through my fingers. I turn to Brett and he is standing with his arms crossed and looking down the road.

The sun lights the granite all the way down it is bright and glowing, the sun against our faces, the wind brushing the tops of pines that line both sides of the road. I hold my hands out and then I pull one arm back, throw everything and then I take the other arm and pull back and everything spills from my hands. The stone bounces into the ditch. The bluebird shatters. The lighters crack. And when everything else lands it is scattered and the wind comes through and holds the receipts the campus map the class schedule the movie stubs the matchbooks the crumpled cigarette packs the plastic leaf tosses them like bodies across the road.

Acknowledgments

Thank you.

Kenneth and Nancy Land. The most amazing parents. Brett and Matthew, who are also Lands, and also the best ever. Howell and Land grandparents. All of whom told me to do what I wanted. Mark and Pat and Zelle and Wilson Land and all their horses and dogs and fields. Deborah and Dow and Elizabeth and Julie Stanley. All other derivations of aunt, uncle and cousin, of which there are many.

These people helped a whole lot.

Sarah Messer, Laura Ford, Jason McLeod, Jynne Martin, Stuart Dybek, Cynthia White, Thisbe Nissen, Matt St. Louis, Rebecca Lee, Jason Skipper, Ken Autrey, Meggen Lyon, Mark Cox, Heather McEntire, Sarah Strickley, Michael White, Justin Lee, Lynn Kostoff, Eric Belk, Jesse Waters, Lia Purpura, Anne Barnehill, JD Dolan, Wes Powell, Wendy Brenner, Jennifer

Abbot, Dave Monahan, Mac Baroody, Philip Gerard, Cody Todd, Denise Gess, Sebastian Matthews, Allyn McLeod, Brian DeVido, Jon Tuttle, Beau Bishop, Rebecca Flanagan, Roy Flanagan, Laura Misco, Dal Conner, Lee Bryant, Stephanie Tewes, Janet Ellerby, David Hisle, Melissa Sanders, John Pritchett, Robyn Morgan, Catherine McCall, Sarah McIntee, Laurel Snyder, Alan Wise, Nick Flynn, Eli Hastings, Terry Tempest Williams, Haven Kimmel, Arlo Crawford, Jessica Craig, Tom Perry, Dan Menaker, Libby McGuire, Robbin Schiff, Paul Kozlowski, Webb Younce, Annie Klein, Steve Messina, David Ebershoff, Janet Cooke, Mary Dolan, Amelia Zalcman, and everyone else at Random House.

Bill Clegg is the best and coolest agent in the whole universe.

Lee Boudreaux is the most genius of editors.

G O A T

B r a d   L a n d

A Reader's Guide

Questions for Discussion

1. *Goat* is a memoir teeming with violence. Did you find yourself more shocked by the random violence in the book than by other, sanctioned types of violence? If so, why?

2. Throughout Land's memoir, many characters grapple with the difficulty of fitting in with their peers. What sorts of pressures do you feel are placed on young men and women? Where does this stress come from? What could be done to combat it?

3. In your opinion, is the Greek system in the United States a viable outlet for young men and women? Given the long public history of hazing and abuses at some fraternities and sororities, do you feel the Greek system should be abolished? If not, how could conditions be improved?

4. The narrator is involved in different kinds of violence: Violence is committed against him and he participates, in some ways, in violence toward others. Identify some places in the text where the author falls into that violence himself, where he becomes part of it.

5. Is Land's character sympathetic in his passivity, and in the detached way he sees the world? Or does this passivity make him less sympathetic?

6. In your opinion, is Land making a claim about the nature of the relationship between different forms of violence in society, such as violent crimes and fraternity hazing? Or is he simply telling a story and allowing the reader to formulate his or her own opinion about this relationship? If so, what is the relationship?

7. Brad's relationship with his younger brother, Brett, is integral to the narrative. What in their relationship does the author find so compelling, so powerful, that he constantly moves toward Brett and seeks his approval in one way or another? Could Brett have done anything differently to protect Brad from his own self-destruction? What could Brad have done differently to change what happened to himself? What is your reaction to the close, almost suffocating nature of the sibling relationship between Brad and Brett?

8. *Goat* is greatly concerned with guilt and forgiveness. In what ways do the violent acts committed against the narrator cause one to think about forgiveness? In what ways do Brett's guilt and his apparent inability to deal with the things that happen to Brad cause him to feel unable to ask for forgiveness?

9. There are many scenes in the book in which Brad is participating in an act of hazing or some other fraternity ritual and Brett is off to the side, in a corner, unable to watch or participate. How does this apparent refusal to help, to recognize what Brad is going through, implicate Brett ethically? Furthermore, how does this affect our beliefs about third parties and forgiveness? Are third parties who choose not to intervene when violence is taking place implicated in those violent acts, and, if so, to what extent?

10. Considering the guilt Brett feels for not being present in his brother's time of need, how is the relationship between Brad and

Brett mirrored in Brad's relationship with Will Fitch? What is it about this relationship that is so compelling, and how does it compel Brad to think about his relationship with his brother?

11. How is this memoir different in form, structure, and tone from other memoirs you've read? Which styles do you feel are more compelling than others?

12. Realizing the inherent difficulty of writing a memoir of this sort, do you consider the voice Land cultivates authentic? In order to remain completely honest with regard to the narrative, the author of any memoir must tell the story as it unfolded—but in doing so, the author always runs the risk of making the wrong choices and sounding too vulnerable or emotionally inhibited. Given the inherent difficulty of exposing oneself in a radical way, do you think Land is successful?

13. Authors of memoirs portray other people's actions from their own perspective, often without asking permission. Does this compromise memoir authors ethically?

14. Early in the book, Land has a conversation with a fox. How can one *really* have a conversation with a fox? What does the inclusion of a scene in a memoir that is at first glance presumably *untrue* imply about the nature of truth-telling?

15. Is there such a thing as an objective claim about the past? How can any author really retrieve the past as it happened, without having to rely solely on memory? If an author uses interviews, for example, does the presence of a tape recorder or microphone, or the very recognition of the fact that the author is listening intently, always compromise the objectivity of what interviewees have to say? Is complete objectivity even possible?

ABOUT THE AUTHOR

BRAD LAND studied creative writing at the
University of North Carolina at Wilmington,
where he received his M.F.A., and Western
Michigan University, where he served as nonfiction editor of *Third Coast*. He has been a
fellow at the MacDowell Colony and now
lives in South Carolina.